SAXON MATH

Course 2

Stephen Hake

Course Assessments

™

A Harcourt Achieve Imprint

www.SaxonPublishers.com

1-800-284-7019

ISBN 13: 978-1-5914-1862-7

Printed in the United States of America

3 4 5 6 7 8 9   0928   12 11 10 09

Course Assessments

Saxon Math Course 2 Assessments contains Course Assessments, Cumulative Test Answer Forms, and Test Analysis Forms. Descriptions of these components are provided below.

About the Placement Test

The Placement Test is a fifty-problem test that can be used to help you find the best initial placement for students who are new to the Saxon math program. The test contains selected content from *Math 5/4, Math 6/5, Course 1, Course 2,* and *Course 3*. Placement Test instructions are provided on page 5 of this book. A scoring guide is provided on page 9. **The Placement Test is not intended for use with current Saxon students.**

Placement Test

About the Baseline Test

A multiple-choice Baseline Test for *Saxon Math Course 2* is included. Administer this fifty-problem test once early in the school year to gauge the skills of incoming students. The content covers skills and concepts that are included in the math curriculum of the preceding year.

Baseline Test

About the Power-Up Tests

Power-Up Tests are administered with the Cumulative Test. Each Cumulative Test identifies the Power-Up Test to be taken that day. Every Power-Up Test contains a facts section and a problem-solving section. The Power-Up Tests are designed to assess students' ability to quickly recall basic facts, demonstrate basic skills, implement problem-solving strategies, and communicate mathematical ideas. We suggest timing students on the facts portion of the Power-Up Test, allowing a maximum of three minutes. Students may complete the problem-solving portion of the Power-Up Test at their own pace.

Power-Up Test

About the Cumulative Tests

The Cumulative Tests are available after every five lessons, beginning after Lesson 10. The tests are designed to reward students and to provide teachers with diagnostic information. The cumulative test design allows students to display the skills they have developed, and it fosters confidence that will benefit students when they encounter comprehensive standardized tests.

Cumulative Test

About the Benchmark Tests

Three cumulative Benchmark Tests for *Saxon Math Course 2* are included. Each contains twenty-five multiple-choice problems. To conserve school days, these tests may be used in lieu of Cumulative Tests 6, 12, and 18 which cover content through Lessons 30, 60, and 90 respectively. The Benchmark Tests are designed to measure student comprehension of topics previously introduced in the course. They provide a measure of student progress on a quarterly basis and can help identify concepts for which additional instruction and practice is indicated. The Benchmark Tests also provide additional practice with multiple-choice items. Familiarity with this format will lead to success on standardized assessment tests.

Benchmark Test

About the End-of-Course Exam

The End-of-Course Exam is a comprehensive, fifty-problem, multiple-choice test that assesses student knowledge of the content presented during the course. This cumulative assessment should be administered as late in the year as possible.

Schedule

Administering the Cumulative Tests according to the schedule is essential. Each test is written to follow a specific five-lesson interval in the textbook. Following the schedule allows students sufficient practice on new topics before they are assessed on those topics.

End-of-Course Exam

Cumulative Tests should be given after every fifth lesson, beginning after Lesson 10. The testing schedule is explained in greater detail on page 4 of this book.

Two forms of each test are included, providing the following options:
- Use one form as an original test and the other as a makeup test.
- Use both forms on test day to discourage copying.
- Use one form as an in-class practice (cooperative work acceptable) and the other as the test.

Additional test forms may be created using the *Saxon Math Course 2 Test and Practice Generator*.

Test Day

On test day we recommend three activities:
1. Administer the Power-Up Test indicated in the *Teacher's Manual* (see Cumulative Assessment page) and on the Cumulative Test.
2. Administer the Cumulative Test.
3. Conduct the Performance Task or Activity suggested in the *Teacher's Manual* (see Performance Assessment page).

Performance Assessment masters are located in the *Instructional Masters* book.

Optional Test Solution Answer Forms are located in this book. Each form provides a structure for students to show their work.

To grade the tests, refer to the Cumulative Test Answers or Solutions in the *Solutions Manual*.

Answer Form A

About the Test Solution Answer Forms

This book contains three kinds of answer forms for the Cumulative Tests that you might find useful. These answer forms provide sufficient space for students to record their work on Cumulative Tests.

Answer Form A: Cumulative Test Solutions

This is a double-sided master with a grid background and partitions for recording the solutions to twenty problems.

Answer Form B

Answer Form B: Cumulative Test Solutions

This is a double-sided master with a plain, white background and partitions for recording the solutions to twenty problems.

Answer Form C: Cumulative Test Solutions

This is a single-sided master with partitions for recording the solutions to twenty problems and a separate answer column on the right-hand side.

Answer Form C

About the Test Analysis Forms

The Cumulative Test Analysis Forms are designed to help you track and analyze student performance on the Cumulative Tests.

Class Test Analysis Form A

Beginning with Cumulative Test 1, record those test items that students have missed. By reviewing the column for items that appear repeatedly, you can quickly determine which test items are causing students the most trouble. Update this form after every test to determine for which concepts additional instruction or practice may be necessary.

Class Test Analysis Form

Individual Test Analysis Form B

This form cross-references every Cumulative Test item with the Lesson where the concept was introduced. Complete a separate form after every test for each student who scored below 80%. Circle the corresponding Lesson for every item missed. Not all students will have mastered a new concept at the time it is first assessed. However, if a student has not mastered a concept after repeated practice and assessment, then reteaching is indicated. This form allows you to identify the student's misunderstandings and plan remediation activities.

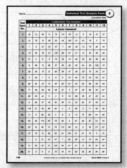

Individual Test Analysis Form

Testing Schedule

Test to be administered:		Covers material through	Give after teaching
Power-Up Test	**Cumulative Test**		
Test 1	Test 1	Lesson 5	Lesson 10
Test 2	Test 2	Lesson 10	Lesson 15
Test 3	Test 3	Lesson 15	Lesson 20
Test 4	Test 4	Lesson 20	Lesson 25
Test 5	Test 5	Lesson 25	Lesson 30
Test 6	Test 6	Lesson 30	Lesson 35
Test 7	Test 7	Lesson 35	Lesson 40
Test 8	Test 8	Lesson 40	Lesson 45
Test 9	Test 9	Lesson 45	Lesson 50
Test 10	Test 10	Lesson 50	Lesson 55
Test 11	Test 11	Lesson 55	Lesson 60
Test 12	Test 12	Lesson 60	Lesson 65
Test 13	Test 13	Lesson 65	Lesson 70
Test 14	Test 14	Lesson 70	Lesson 75
Test 15	Test 15	Lesson 75	Lesson 80
Test 16	Test 16	Lesson 80	Lesson 85
Test 17	Test 17	Lesson 85	Lesson 90
Test 18	Test 18	Lesson 90	Lesson 95
Test 19	Test 19	Lesson 95	Lesson 100
Test 20	Test 20	Lesson 100	Lesson 105
Test 21	Test 21	Lesson 105	Lesson 110
Test 22	Test 22	Lesson 110	Lesson 115
Test 23	Test 23	Lesson 115	Lesson 120

Use this test to help determine correct placement within Saxon's middle grades series.

The following placement test may be of assistance in placing some students. Please note that this test is simply a tool to assist teachers in the initial placement of their students. **This test should not be used to determine whether a student already using the Saxon program should skip a textbook.** Allow the student one hour to take the test (or until he or she cannot work any more problems). The student should work without assistance and show all work. Calculators may not be used during the test.

Look over the student's work carefully, grade the test, and use the guidelines below to place the student. An online version of the placement test is available at www.SaxonPublishers.com.

Placement Test Guide	
4 or fewer correct from Problems 1–10 and student is an average to accelerated fourth-grader	Student may begin *Saxon Math 5/4*.
5 or more correct from Problems 1–10	Student may begin *Saxon Math 6/5*.
7 or more correct from Problems 1–10 and **5 or more correct** from Problems 11–20	Student may begin *Saxon Math Course 1*.
7 or more correct from Problems 11–20 and **5 or more correct** from Problems 21–30	Student may begin *Saxon Math Course 2*.
7 or more correct from Problems 21–30 and **5 or more correct** from Problems 31–40	Student may begin *Saxon Math Course 3*.
7 or more correct from Problems 31–40 and **5 or more correct** from Problems 41–50	Student may begin *Saxon Math Algebra 1*; student may need to take the placement test for Algebra 1.

Problems from Math 5/4

1. Roberta had six quarters, three dimes, and fourteen pennies. How much money did Roberta have?

2. At 11:45 a.m. Jason glanced at his watch. His doctor's appointment was in 2 hours. At what time was the appointment?

3. What fraction of this rectangle is shaded?

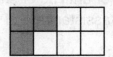

4. What is the perimeter of this rectangle?

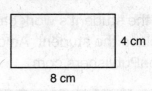

4 cm

8 cm

5. Three feet equals one yard. A car that is 15 feet long is how many yards long?

6. $\begin{array}{r} 346 \\ \times\ \ 90 \\ \hline \end{array}$

7. $\begin{array}{r} \$20.00 \\ -\ \$17.84 \\ \hline \end{array}$

8. $4\overline{)1480}$

9. $48 + 163 + 9 + 83$

10. How long is this line segment?

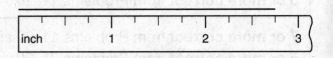

Problems from Math 6/5

11. Carlos gave the clerk a $10 bill for a book that cost $6.95 plus $0.42 tax. How much money should Carlos get back from the clerk?

12. The distance around the school track is $\frac{1}{4}$ mile. How many times around the track does Cheryl need to run in order to run one mile?

13. Estimate the product of 67 and 73 by rounding each number to the nearest ten before multiplying.

14. In 2 hours the 3 boys picked a total of 1347 cherries. If they share the cherries equally, then how many cherries will each boy keep?

 Saxon Math Course 2

15. $\begin{array}{r} 67 \\ \times\ 89 \\ \hline \end{array}$ **16.** $\begin{array}{r} 4608 \\ -\ 2729 \\ \hline \end{array}$ **17.** $60\overline{)1590}$

18. $2.25 + 12.7$ **19.** $5\frac{3}{4} + 2\frac{3}{4}$

20. This rectangle is half as wide as it is long. What is the perimeter of the rectangle?

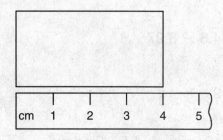

Problems from Course 1

21. New York City uses about one billion, three hundred million gallons of water each day. Use digits to write that number.

22. Jill is on page 42 of a 180-page book. If she must finish the book in three days, then she needs to read an average of how many pages each day?

23. Carol cut $2\frac{1}{2}$ inches off her hair three times last year. If she had not cut her hair, how much longer would it have been at the end of the year?

24. One half of the area of the square is shaded. What is the area of the shaded region?

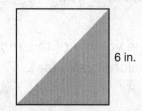

6 in.

25. $2\frac{1}{3} + 1\frac{3}{4}$ **26.** 6.3×0.48 **27.** $6.7 + 0.48$

28. $\frac{5}{8} \times \frac{3}{5}$ **29.** $6.3 \div 9$

30. If $n - 72 = 36$, what is the value of n?

Problems from Course 2

31. Round 27,647 to the nearest thousand.

32. Forty percent of the thirty students in the class are boys. How many girls are in the class?

33. Evaluate $ab - c$ if $a = 5$, $b = 3$, and $c = 4$.

34. Albert bought 3 blank tapes for $5.95. Find the cost per tape to the nearest cent.

35. $4.6 - 3.97$

36. $2.5 \div 100$

37. $2\frac{1}{2} \times 1\frac{2}{3}$

38. $\frac{3}{4} \div \frac{2}{3}$

39. $10 - w = 1.5$ Find w.

40. What is the area of this triangle?

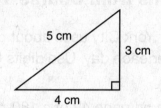

Problems from Course 3

41. What fraction of 56 is 21?

42. What number is $\frac{4}{7}$ of 210?

43. Evaluate $xy - yt$ if $x = 12$, $y = \frac{1}{3}$, and $t = 6$.

44. Find the volume of this rectangular solid. Dimensions are in feet.

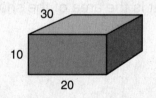

45. Find the area of this figure. Dimensions are in centimeters.

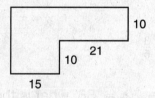

46. $(-5)(-3) + (-6)$

47. 18.4×0.013

48. $\frac{7}{8} + 1\frac{3}{16} - \frac{1}{2}$

49. $5x - 2 = 88$ Find x.

50. $(6)(3) + 4(2 + 12)$

Saxon Math Course 2

Name _____   Recommended placement _____

Grade _____   School _____

Date tested _____

Directions: For each correct answer, place a check mark in the corresponding box. For each section, count the number of correct answers. Place the student according to the placement information for that section.

Scorecard	Number of Correct Answers	Placement

1. ☐ 2. ☐
3. ☐ 4. ☐
5. ☐ 6. ☐
7. ☐ 8. ☐
9. ☐ 10. ☐
	_____	**Four or fewer correct from 1–10:**
		 1. Average-to-accelerated fourth grader:
		    Begin *Math 5/4*.
		 2. Below average fourth grader:
		    Consider *Math 3*.
		Five or more correct from 1–10:
		 Begin *Math 6/5*.

11. ☐ 12. ☐ 13. ☐ 14. ☐ 15. ☐ 16. ☐ 17. ☐ 18. ☐ 19. ☐ 20. ☐	_____	**Seven or more correct from 1–10 and five or more correct from 11–20:** Begin *Course 1*.
21. ☐ 22. ☐ 23. ☐ 24. ☐ 25. ☐ 26. ☐ 27. ☐ 28. ☐ 29. ☐ 30. ☐	_____	**Seven or more correct from 11–20 and five or more correct from 21–30:** Begin *Course 2*.
31. ☐ 32. ☐ 33. ☐ 34. ☐ 35. ☐ 36. ☐ 37. ☐ 38. ☐ 39. ☐ 40. ☐	_____	**Seven or more correct from 21–30 and five or more correct from 31–40:** Begin *Course 3*.
41. ☐ 42. ☐ 43. ☐ 44. ☐ 45. ☐ 46. ☐ 47. ☐ 48. ☐ 49. ☐ 50. ☐	_____	**Seven or more correct from 31–40 and five or more correct from 41–50:** Student may begin *Algebra 1* or may need to take the placement test for *Algebra 1*.

1. $1.94

2. 2:15 p.m.

3. $\frac{3}{8}$

4. 24 cm

5. 5 yards

6. 31,140

7. $2.16

8. 370

9. 303

10. $2\frac{3}{4}$

11. $2.63

12. 4 times

13. 4900

14. 449 cherries

15. 5963

16. 1879

17. 26 R 30 or $26\frac{1}{2}$ or 26.5

18. 14.95

19. $8\frac{1}{2}$

20. 12 cm

21. 1,300,000,000

22. 46 pages

23. $7\frac{1}{2}$ in.

24. 18 sq. in. or 18 in.^{2}

25. $4\frac{1}{12}$

26. 3.024

27. 7.18

28. $\frac{3}{8}$

29. 0.7

30. 108

31. 28,000

32. 18 girls

33. 11

34. $1.98

35. 0.63

36. 0.025

37. $4\frac{1}{6}$

38. $1\frac{1}{8}$

39. 8.5

40. 6 cm^2

41. $\frac{3}{8}$

42. 120

43. 2

44. 6000 ft^3

45. 510 cm^2

46. 9

47. 0.2392

48. $1\frac{9}{16}$

49. 18

50. 74

Saxon Math Course

Name _____

1. 7610 ÷ 25 equals

    A. $34\frac{2}{5}$ **B.** $340\frac{2}{5}$ **C.** $304\frac{2}{5}$ **D.** $300\frac{2}{5}$ **E.** None correct

2. 8.75 + 6 + 4.5 equals

    A. 18.25   **B.** 9.26   **C.** 13.31   **D.** 19.25   **E.** None correct

3. 1.8 – 0.25 equals

    A. 1.55   **B.** 1.65   **C.** 1.3   **D.** 0.7   **E.** None correct

4. 0.15 × 4.2 equals

    A. 0.63   **B.** 6.3   **C.** 630   **D.** 0.063   **E.** None correct

5. 3.64 ÷ 0.7 equals

    A. 0.52   **B.** 5.2   **C.** 52   **D.** 520   **E.** None correct

6. $1\frac{2}{3} + 2\frac{5}{6}$ equals

    A. $3\frac{7}{9}$ **B.** $4\frac{1}{2}$ **C.** $3\frac{1}{2}$ **D.** $4\frac{1}{6}$ **E.** None correct

7. $3\frac{2}{5} - 1\frac{1}{2}$ equals

    A. $2\frac{1}{3}$ **B.** $2\frac{1}{10}$ **C.** $1\frac{9}{10}$ **D.** $4\frac{9}{10}$ **E.** None correct

8. $\frac{4}{5} \times 3\frac{1}{3}$ equals

    A. $3\frac{4}{15}$ **B.** $1\frac{13}{15}$ **C.** $2\frac{2}{3}$ **D.** $\frac{3}{25}$ **E.** None correct

9. $2\frac{2}{5} \div 1\frac{1}{2}$ equals

    A. $1\frac{3}{5}$ **B.** $2\frac{1}{2}$ **C.** $3\frac{3}{5}$ **D.** $\frac{5}{8}$ **E.** None correct

10. $\frac{60}{84}$, reduced to lowest terms, is

    A. $\frac{15}{21}$ **B.** $\frac{30}{42}$ **C.** $\frac{5}{7}$ **D.** $\frac{1}{2}$ **E.** None correct

11. Which digit in 64,327.891 is in the thousands place?

    A. 6   **B.** 4   **C.** 9   **D.** 1   **E.** None correct

12. $2\frac{1}{2}$ million is

    A. 2,500,000   **B.** 2,500,000,000

    C. $2,000,000\frac{1}{2}$ **D.** 2,200,000   **E.** None correct

13. Which of these equals 1.2 m?

    A. 1200 cm   **B.** 0.12 km   **C.** 1200 mm   **D.** 12 m   **E.** None correct

14. Which is the most reasonable measure for the length of a bicycle?

    A. 2 mm   **B.** 2 m   **C.** 2 cm   **D.** 2 km

15. 40% is NOT equivalent to

    A. 0.4   **B.** $\frac{2}{5}$ **C.** $\frac{40}{100}$ **D.** 0.04

Saxon Math Course 2

16. $10^3 \cdot 10^4$ equals

    A. 10^{12} **B.** 10^7 **C.** 1 million   **D.** 1200   **E.** None correct

17. $\sqrt{199}$ is between

    A. 99 and 100   **B.** 9 and 10

    C. 14 and 15   **D.** 19 and 20   **E.** None correct

18. Twenty-five thousandths may be written as

    A. 0.25   **B.** 25,000   **C.** 20,005   **D.** 20.005   **E.** None correct

19. Estimate the sum of 17.36 and 8.7 by rounding each decimal number to the nearest whole number before adding.

    A. 9   **B.** 17   **C.** 25   **D.** 26   **E.** None correct

20. Which set of numbers is arranged in order from least to greatest?

    A. 33%, $\frac{1}{3}$, 0.3   **B.** 0.3, $\frac{1}{3}$, 33%

    C. 0.3, 33%, $\frac{1}{3}$ **D.** $\frac{1}{3}$, 0.3, $3\frac{1}{3}$ **E.** None correct

21. What number solves this proportion? $\dfrac{8}{12} = \dfrac{12}{n}$

    A. 8   **B.** 16   **C.** 18   **D.** 24   **E.** None correct

22. The ratio of boys to girls in the class was 2 to 3. If there were 18 girls in the class, how many students were in the class?

    A. 12   **B.** 24   **C.** 27   **D.** 30   **E.** None correct

23. The average age of three people is 25. If two of the people are 22, how old is the third person?

    A. 23   **B.** 25   **C.** 28   **D.** 31   **E.** None correct

24. Ten children measured how high they could jump. The results they recorded, in inches, were as follows:

$$8, 9, 8, 6, 8, 12, 9, 10, 11, 16$$

What is the median of these measures?

    A. 8 in.   **B.** 9 in.   **C.** 9.5 in.   **D.** 10 in.   **E.** None correct

25. One white marble, two red marbles, and three blue marbles are in a bag. What is the probability of drawing a blue marble from the bag?

    A. $\frac{1}{6}$ **B.** $\frac{1}{3}$ **C.** $\frac{1}{2}$ **D.** $\frac{3}{5}$ **E.** None correct

26. If the price of an item is $2.89 and the sales-tax rate is 8%, what is the total cost of the item including sales tax?

    A. $2.97   **B.** $3.12   **C.** $3.17   **D.** $23.12   **E.** None correct

27. What is the price per ounce of a 32-ounce box of cereal that costs $4.16?

    A. 11¢/oz   **B.** 12¢/oz   **C.** 13¢/oz   **D.** 16¢/oz   **E.** None correct

28. A shirt regularly priced at $36.00 was on sale for 25% off. What was the sale price?

    A. $9.00   **B.** $24.00   **C.** $27.00   **D.** $48.00   **E.** None correct

29. Emma correctly answered 21 of the 25 questions. What percent of the questions did Emma answer correctly?

   A. 21%   **B.** 84%   **C.** 16%   **D.** 96%   **E.** None correct

30. At a constant speed of 400 miles per hour, how far can an airplane fly in $2\frac{1}{2}$ hours?

   A. 600 miles   **B.** 800 miles   **C.** 650 miles   **D.** 1000 miles   **E.** None correct

31. Which of these triangles appears to be equilateral?

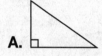

A.   **B.**

C.   **D.**

   E. None correct

32. If ∠x measures 38° in this triangle, what is the measure of ∠y?

   A. 52°   **B.** 62°   **C.** 38°   **D.** 142°   **E.** None correct

33. What is the perimeter of this figure? All angles are right angles.

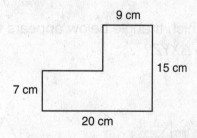

   A. 212 cm   **B.** 67 cm   **C.** 51 cm   **D.** 70 cm   **E.** None correct

34. If the radius of a bicycle tire is 10 inches, what is the tire's circumference? (Use 3.14 for π.)

    A. 31.4 in.   **B.** 62.8 in.   **C.** 314 in.   **D.** 20 in.   **E.** None correct

35. What is the area of this triangle?

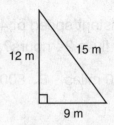

    A. 108 m²   **B.** 54 m²   **C.** 36 m   **D.** 108 m   **E.** None correct

36. The diameter of a circular braided rug is 8 feet. Which choice best approximates the area covered by the rug?

    A. 50 ft²   **B.** 25 ft²   **C.** 64 ft²   **D.** 16 ft²

37. What is the volume of this small box?

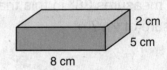

    A. 80 cm³   **B.** 40 cm³   **C.** 30 cm³   **D.** 15 cm³   **E.** None correct

38. Which triangle below appears to be similar to △XYZ?

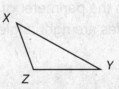

       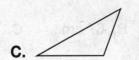

A.   **B.**   **C.**   **D.**

Saxon Math Course

39. In rectangle QRST, which segment is parallel to $\overline{QR}$?

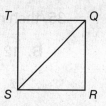

A. $\overline{QS}$ B. $\overline{QT}$ C. $\overline{RS}$ D. $\overline{TS}$ E. None correct

40. If $3^2 + 4^2 = c^2$, then which of these could be the value of c?

A. 5   B. 7   C. 25   D. 49   E. None correct

41. $(-6) + (-3) + (+2)$ equals

A. −5   B. −7   C. −1   D. −11   E. None correct

42. If a is 3 and c is 12, then $4ac$ equals

A. 19   B. 36   C. 4312   D. 144   E. None correct

43. $3[16 - 2(5 - 3)]$ equals

A. 9   B. 35   C. 36   D. 44   E. None correct

44. The prime factorization of 24 may be written as

A. $2^3 \cdot 3$ B. $2 \cdot 12$ C. $3 \cdot 8$ D. $6 \cdot 4$ E. None correct

45. $6(25)$ equals

A. $6 \cdot 20 \cdot 5$ B. $6 \cdot 24 + 5$ C. $6 \cdot 20 + 5$ D. $6 \cdot 20 + 6 \cdot 5$

46. If $3m - 1 = 35$, then m equals

    A. 6   **B.** 12   **C.** 34   **D.** 36   **E.** None correct

47. Which of these inequalities states that the square root of 9 is less than 2 squared?

    A. $\sqrt{9} < 2^2$ **B.** $\sqrt{9} > 2^2$ **C.** $9^2 < \sqrt{2}$ **D.** $9^2 > \sqrt{2}$ **E.** None correct

48. $(-10)(-10)$ equals

    A. −100   **B.** 100   **C.** −20   **D.** 0   **E.** None correct

49. Find the missing number in the function table.

x	3	5	8
$2x - 3$	3	7	?

    A. 10   **B.** 11   **C.** 12   **D.** 13   **E.** None correct

50. The coordinates of three vertices of a rectangle are $(-2, 3)$, $(4, 3)$, and $(4, -3)$. The coordinates of the fourth vertex are

    A. $(-2, -3)$ **B.** $(4, -2)$ **C.** $(-2, 4)$ **D.** $(-3, 3)$ **E.** None correct

Saxon Math Course 2

Name _____ Time _____

Facts	Multiply.								
9 $\times 8$	8 $\times 2$	10 $\times 10$	6 $\times 3$	4 $\times 2$	5 $\times 5$	9 $\times 9$	6 $\times 4$	9 $\times 6$	7 $\times 3$
9 $\times 3$	6 $\times 5$	0 $\times 0$	7 $\times 6$	8 $\times 8$	7 $\times 4$	5 $\times 3$	9 $\times 7$	2 $\times 2$	8 $\times 6$
7 $\times 7$	6 $\times 2$	4 $\times 3$	8 $\times 5$	4 $\times 4$	3 $\times 2$	n $\times 0$	8 $\times 4$	6 $\times 6$	9 $\times 2$
8 $\times 3$	5 $\times 4$	n $\times 1$	7 $\times 2$	9 $\times 5$	8 $\times 7$	3 $\times 3$	9 $\times 4$	5 $\times 2$	7 $\times 5$

Problem Solving	Answer the question below.

Problem: Kids on a field trip to a dairy farm are gathered in the barn with cows. If there are 11 heads and 28 legs in the barn, how many kids and how many cows are in the barn?

Understand
What information am I given?
What am I asked to find or do?

- -

Plan
How can I use the information I am given?
Which strategy should I try?

- -

Solve
Did I follow the plan?
Did I show my work?
Did I write the answer?

- -

Check
Did I use the correct information?
Did I do what was asked?
Is my answer reasonable?

Name _____ Time _____

Math Course 2

Facts   Solve each equation.

$a + 12 = 20$	$b - 8 = 10$	$5c = 40$	$\dfrac{d}{4} = 12$	$11 + e = 24$
$a =$	$b =$	$c =$	$d =$	$e =$
$25 - f = 10$	$10g = 60$	$\dfrac{24}{h} = 6$	$15 = j + 8$	$20 = k - 5$
$f =$	$g =$	$h =$	$j =$	$k =$
$30 = 6m$	$9 = \dfrac{n}{3}$	$18 = 6 + p$	$5 = 15 - q$	$36 = 4r$
$m =$	$n =$	$p =$	$q =$	$r =$
$2 = \dfrac{16}{s}$	$t + 8 = 12$	$u - 15 = 30$	$8v = 48$	$\dfrac{w}{3} = 6$
$s =$	$t =$	$u =$	$v =$	$w =$

Problem Solving   Answer the question below.

Problem: An art teacher makes earrings from silver nuggets. Each nugget makes 1 earring. The shavings left over from 6 nuggets are then melted and recast to form one more nugget. The teacher ordered 36 nuggets for her class. How many earrings can be made from 36 nuggets?

Understand
What information am I given?
What am I asked to find or do?

Plan
How can I use the information I am given?
Which strategy should I try?

Solve
Did I follow the plan?
Did I show my work?
Did I write the answer?

Check
Did I use the correct information?
Did I do what was asked?
Is my answer reasonable?

     Saxon Math Course 2

Facts	Write each improper fraction as a whole number or mixed number.			
$\frac{5}{2} =$	$\frac{7}{4} =$	$\frac{12}{5} =$	$\frac{10}{3} =$	$\frac{15}{2} =$
$\frac{15}{5} =$	$\frac{11}{8} =$	$2\frac{3}{2} =$	$4\frac{5}{4} =$	$3\frac{7}{4} =$

Write each mixed number as an improper fraction.

$1\frac{1}{2} =$	$2\frac{2}{3} =$	$3\frac{3}{4} =$	$2\frac{1}{2} =$	$6\frac{2}{3} =$
$2\frac{3}{4} =$	$3\frac{1}{3} =$	$4\frac{1}{2} =$	$1\frac{7}{8} =$	$12\frac{1}{2} =$

Problem Solving   Answer the question below.

Problem: Sarah remembered that the three numbers she used to open her combination lock were 32, 16, and 8, but she could not remember the order. List all the permutations (arrangements) of the three numbers Sarah could try.

Understand
What information am I given?
What am I asked to find or do?

- -

Plan
How can I use the information I am given?
Which strategy should I try?

- -

Solve
Did I follow the plan?
Did I show my work?
Did I write the answer?

- -

Check
Did I use the correct information?
Did I do what was asked?
Is my answer reasonable?

Facts   Reduce each fraction to lowest terms.

$\frac{50}{100} =$	$\frac{4}{16} =$	$\frac{6}{8} =$	$\frac{8}{12} =$	$\frac{10}{100} =$
$\frac{8}{16} =$	$\frac{20}{100} =$	$\frac{3}{12} =$	$\frac{60}{100} =$	$\frac{9}{12} =$
$\frac{6}{9} =$	$\frac{90}{100} =$	$\frac{5}{10} =$	$\frac{12}{16} =$	$\frac{25}{100} =$
$\frac{4}{10} =$	$\frac{4}{6} =$	$\frac{75}{100} =$	$\frac{4}{12} =$	$\frac{6}{10} =$

Problem Solving   Answer the question below.

Problem: A bookworm finds itself on page 1 of volume 1, and begins eating straight through to the last page of volume 5. The volumes are in order on the shelf, and each book is 6 cm thick, including the front and back covers, which are each $\frac{1}{2}$ cm thick. How far will the bookworm travel?

Understand
What information am I given?
What am I asked to find or do?

- -

Plan
How can I use the information I am given?
Which strategy should I try?

- -

Solve
Did I follow the plan?
Did I show my work?
Did I write the answer?

- -

Check
Did I use the correct information?
Did I do what was asked?
Is my answer reasonable?

Name _____ Time _____

Facts   Write the word or words to complete each definition.

The distance around a circle is its _____ .	Every point on a circle is the same distance from its _____ .	The distance across a circle through it's center is its _____ .	The distance from a circle to it's center is its _____ .
Two or more circles with the same center are _____ .	A segment between two points on a circle is a _____ .	Part of a circumference is an _____ .	Part of a circle bounded by an arc and two radii is a _____ .
Half a circle is a _____ .	An angle whose vertex is the center of a circle is a _____ .	An angle whose vertex is on the circle whose sides include chords is an _____ .	A polygon whose vertices are on the circle and whose edges are within the circle is an _____ .

Problem Solving   Answer the question below.

Problem: Fiona has 8 coins totaling 50¢. What combinations of coins could Fiona have?

Understand
What information am I given?
What am I asked to find or do?

- -

Plan
How can I use the information I am given?
Which strategy should I try?

- -

Solve
Did I follow the plan?
Did I show my work?
Did I write the answer?

- -

Check
Did I use the correct information?
Did I do what was asked?
Is my answer reasonable?

Name _____ Time _____

Facts	Name each figure illustrated.		
1. _____	2. _____	3. _____	4. _____
5. _____	6. _____	7. _____	8. _____
9. _____	10. _____	11. _____	12. A polygon whose sides are equal in length and whose angles are equal in measure is a _____.

Problem Solving	Answer the question below.

Problem: Copy this problem and find the missing digits.
No two digits may be alike.

$$\begin{array}{r} \_\ \_\ \_ \\ \times\quad\ 7 \\ \hline 9\ \_\ \_ \end{array}$$

Understand
What information am I given?
What am I asked to find or do?

- -

Plan
How can I use the information I am given?
Which strategy should I try?

- -

Solve
Did I follow the plan?
Did I show my work?
Did I write the answer?

- -

Check
Did I use the correct information?
Did I do what was asked?
Is my answer reasonable?

Facts   Simplify.

$\frac{2}{3} + \frac{2}{3} =$	$\frac{2}{3} - \frac{1}{3} =$	$\frac{2}{3} \times \frac{2}{3} =$	$\frac{2}{3} \div \frac{2}{3} =$
$\frac{3}{4} + \frac{1}{4} =$	$\frac{3}{4} - \frac{1}{4} =$	$\frac{3}{4} \times \frac{1}{4} =$	$\frac{3}{4} \div \frac{1}{4} =$
$\frac{2}{3} + \frac{1}{2} =$	$\frac{2}{3} - \frac{1}{2} =$	$\frac{2}{3} \times \frac{1}{2} =$	$\frac{2}{3} \div \frac{1}{2} =$
$\frac{3}{4} + \frac{2}{3} =$	$\frac{3}{4} - \frac{2}{3} =$	$\frac{3}{4} \times \frac{2}{3} =$	$\frac{3}{4} \div \frac{2}{3} =$

Problem Solving   Answer the question below.

Problem: A quart is half of a half-gallon. A pint is half of a quart. A cup is half of a pint. If milk from a full gallon container is used to fill empty half-gallon, quart, pint and cup containers, how much milk will be left in the gallon container?

Understand
What information am I given?
What am I asked to find or do?

Plan
How can I use the information I am given?
Which strategy should I try?

Solve
Did I follow the plan?
Did I show my work?
Did I write the answer?

Check
Did I use the correct information?
Did I do what was asked?
Is my answer reasonable?

Facts   Write the number that completes each equivalent measure.   *Math Course 2*

1. 1 foot	= _____	inches
2. 1 yard	= _____	inches
3. 1 yard	= _____	feet
4. 1 mile	= _____	feet
5. 1 centimeter	= _____	millimeters
6. 1 meter	= _____	millimeters
7. 1 meter	= _____	centimeters
8. 1 kilometer	= _____	meters
9. 1 inch	= _____	centimeters
10. 1 pound	= _____	ounces
11. 1 ton	= _____	pounds
12. 1 gram	= _____	milligrams
13. 1 kilogram	= _____	grams
14. 1 metric ton	= _____	kilograms

15. 1 kilogram	≈ _____	pounds
16. 1 pint	= _____	ounces
17. 1 pint	= _____	cups
18. 1 quart	= _____	pints
19. 1 gallon	= _____	quarts
20. 1 liter	= _____	milliliters

21–24. 1 milliliter of water has a volume of _____ and a mass of _____ .
One liter of water has a volume of _____ cm^3 and a mass of _____ kg.

25–26. Water freezes at _____ °F and _____ °C.

27–28. Water boils at _____ °F and _____ °C.

29–30. Normal body temperature is _____ °F and _____ °C.

Problem Solving   Answer the question below.

Problem: If 2 chickens can lay a total of 2 eggs in 2 days, how many eggs can 4 chickens lay in 4 days?

Understand
What information am I given?
What am I asked to find or do?

Plan
How can I use the information I am given?
Which strategy should I try?

Solve
Did I follow the plan?
Did I show my work?
Did I write the answer?

Check
Did I use the correct information?
Did I do what was asked?
Is my answer reasonable?

   Saxon Math Course 2

Name _____ Time _____

Facts   Find the number that completes each proportion.

$\frac{3}{4} = \frac{a}{12}$	$\frac{3}{4} = \frac{12}{b}$	$\frac{c}{5} = \frac{12}{20}$	$\frac{2}{d} = \frac{12}{24}$	$\frac{8}{12} = \frac{4}{e}$
$\frac{f}{10} = \frac{10}{5}$	$\frac{5}{g} = \frac{25}{100}$	$\frac{10}{100} = \frac{5}{h}$	$\frac{8}{4} = \frac{j}{16}$	$\frac{24}{k} = \frac{8}{6}$
$\frac{9}{12} = \frac{36}{m}$	$\frac{50}{100} = \frac{w}{30}$	$\frac{3}{9} = \frac{5}{p}$	$\frac{q}{60} = \frac{15}{20}$	$\frac{2}{5} = \frac{r}{100}$

Problem Solving   Answer the question below.

Problem: Two children want to build a triangular dog pen in a corner of their backyard for their dog. They have 100 feet of fencing. They stretch 55 feet of fencing diagonally across the corner of the yard. What can you predict about the rest of the fencing project?

Understand
What information am I given?
What am I asked to find or do?

Plan
How can I use the information I am given?
Which strategy should I try?

Solve
Did I follow the plan?
Did I show my work?
Did I write the answer?

Check
Did I use the correct information?
Did I do what was asked?
Is my answer reasonable?

Facts Simplify.			
0.8 + 0.4 =	0.8 − 0.4 =	0.8 × 0.4 =	0.8 ÷ 0.4 =
1.2 + 0.4 =	1.2 − 0.4 =	1.2 × 0.4 =	1.2 ÷ 0.4 =
6 + 0.3 =	6 − 0.3 =	6 × 0.3 =	6 ÷ 0.3 =
1.2 + 4 =	0.01 − 0.01 =	0.3 × 0.3 =	0.12 ÷ 4 =

Problem Solving   Answer the question below.

Problem: Mariabella was $\frac{1}{4}$ of the way through her book. Twenty pages later she was $\frac{1}{3}$ of the way through her book. When she is $\frac{3}{4}$ of the way through the book, how many pages will she have to read to finish the book?

Understand
What information am I given?
What am I asked to find or do?

- -

Plan
How can I use the information I am given?
Which strategy should I try?

- -

Solve
Did I follow the plan?
Did I show my work?
Did I write the answer?

- -

Check
Did I use the correct information?
Did I do what was asked?
Is my answer reasonable?

         Saxon Math Course 2

Facts	Simplify each power or root.			
$\sqrt{100} =$	$\sqrt{16} =$	$\sqrt{81} =$	$\sqrt{4} =$	$\sqrt{144} =$
$\sqrt{64} =$	$\sqrt{49} =$	$\sqrt{25} =$	$\sqrt{9} =$	$\sqrt{36} =$
$8^2 =$	$5^2 =$	$3^2 =$	$12^2 =$	$10^2 =$
$7^2 =$	$2^3 =$	$3^3 =$	$10^3 =$	$5^3 =$

Problem Solving Answer the question below.

Problem: The captain told Alexa that a lobster's age in years is approximately its weight multiplied by 4, plus three years. Write the captain's statement as an equation. About how much will a 13-year-old lobster weigh? What is the approximate age of a lobster that weighs 6 pounds?

Understand
What information am I given?
What am I asked to find or do?

Plan
How can I use the information I am given?
Which strategy should I try?

Solve
Did I follow the plan?
Did I show my work?
Did I write the answer?

Check
Did I use the correct information?
Did I do what was asked?
Is my answer reasonable?

Facts Write the equivalent decimal and percent for each fraction. *Math Course 2*

Fraction	Decimal	Percent	Fraction	Decimal	Percent
$\frac{1}{2}$			$\frac{1}{8}$		
$\frac{1}{3}$			$\frac{1}{10}$		
$\frac{2}{3}$			$\frac{3}{10}$		
$\frac{1}{4}$			$\frac{9}{10}$		
$\frac{3}{4}$			$\frac{1}{100}$		
$\frac{1}{5}$			$1\frac{1}{2}$		

Problem Solving Answer the question below.

Problem: Marsha started a 1024-meter race, ran half the distance to the finish line, and then handed the baton to Greg. Greg ran half the remaining distance and handed off to Alice, who ran half the remaining distance. How far from the finish line did Alice stop? If the team continues this pattern, how many more runners will they need in order to cross the finish line?

Understand
What information am I given?
What am I asked to find or do?

Plan
How can I use the information I am given?
Which strategy should I try?

Solve
Did I follow the plan?
Did I show my work?
Did I write the answer?

Check
Did I use the correct information?
Did I do what was asked?
Is my answer reasonable?

Facts	Write the number for each conversion or factor.

1. 2 m = _____ cm

2. 1.5 km = _____ m

3. 2.54 cm = _____ mm

4. 125 cm = _____ m

5. 10 km = _____ m

6. 5000 m = _____ km

7. 50 cm = _____ m

8. 50 cm = _____ mm

9. 2 L = _____ mL

10. 250 mL = _____ L

11. 4 kg = _____ g

12. 2.5 g = _____ mg

13. 500 mg = _____ g

14. 0.5 kg = _____ g

15–16. Two liters of water have a volume of _____ cm^3 and a mass of ___ kg.

	Prefix	Factor
17.	kilo-	
18.	hecto-	
19.	deka-	
	(unit)	
20.	deci-	
21.	centi-	
22.	milli-	

Problem Solving	Answer the question below.

Problem: Two sisters, Gaby and Natalia, decide to buy a computer together. Natalia earns money helping the girls' grandparents. Gaby is older and has a full-time job for the summer. Because Gaby will be earning three times as much as her sister, she says that Natalia should pay for $\frac{1}{4}$ of the computer. Natalia thinks she should pay for $\frac{1}{3}$ of the computer. Who is correct?

Understand
What information am I given?
What am I asked to find or do?

Plan
How can I use the information I am given?
Which strategy should I try?

Solve
Did I follow the plan?
Did I show my work?
Did I write the answer?

Check
Did I use the correct information?
Did I do what was asked?
Is my answer reasonable?

Name _____ Time _____

Power-Up Test 1

Math Course 2

Facts   Simplify. Reduce the answers if possible.

$3 + 1\frac{2}{3} =$	$3 - 1\frac{2}{3} =$	$3 \times 1\frac{2}{3} =$	$3 \div 1\frac{2}{3} =$
$1\frac{2}{3} + 1\frac{1}{2} =$	$1\frac{2}{3} - 1\frac{1}{2} =$	$1\frac{2}{3} \times 1\frac{1}{2} =$	$1\frac{2}{3} \div 1\frac{1}{2} =$
$2\frac{1}{2} + 1\frac{2}{3} =$	$2\frac{1}{2} - 1\frac{2}{3} =$	$2\frac{1}{2} \times 1\frac{2}{3} =$	$2\frac{1}{2} \div 1\frac{2}{3} =$
$4\frac{1}{2} + 2\frac{1}{4} =$	$4\frac{1}{2} - 2\frac{1}{4} =$	$4\frac{1}{2} \times 2\frac{1}{4} =$	$4\frac{1}{2} \div 2\frac{1}{4} =$

Problem Solving   Answer the question below.

Problem: One-foot-square tiles, packed 20 per box, will be used to cover the floor of a rectangular room. The room is 20 ft 6 in. long and 14 ft 6 in. wide. If all cut-off portions of tiles can be used, how many boxes of tile are needed? If only one portion from each cut tile may be used, how many boxes are needed?

Understand
What information am I given?
What am I asked to find or do?

Plan
How can I use the information I am given?
Which strategy should I try?

Solve
Did I follow the plan?
Did I show my work?
Did I write the answer?

Check
Did I use the correct information?
Did I do what was asked?
Is my answer reasonable?

32   © Harcourt Achieve Inc. and Stephen Hake. All rights reserved.   *Saxon Math* Course 2

Facts   Select from the words below to describe each figure.

1.	2.	3.	4.
_____	_____	_____	_____
_____	_____	_____	_____
_____			_____

5.	6.	7.	8.
_____	_____	_____	_____
_____	_____	_____	_____

kite	rectangle	isosceles triangle	right triangle
trapezoid	rhombus	scalene triangle	acute triangle
parallelogram	square	equilateral triangle	obtuse triangle

Problem Solving   Answer the question below.

Problem: Telephone poles, spaced 100 feet apart, line the road on which Jesse lives. If Jesse runs from the first pole to the seventh pole, how many feet does he run? Draw a picture that illustrates the problem.

Understand
What information am I given?
What am I asked to find or do?

Plan
How can I use the information I am given?
Which strategy should I try?

Solve
Did I follow the plan?
Did I show my work?
Did I write the answer?

Check
Did I use the correct information?
Did I do what was asked?
Is my answer reasonable?

Facts Simplify.			
$(-8) + (-2) =$	$(-8) - (-2) =$	$(-8)(-2) =$	$\dfrac{-8}{-2} =$
$(-9) + (+3) =$	$(-9) - (+3) =$	$(-9)(+3) =$	$\dfrac{-9}{+3} =$
$12 + (-2) =$	$12 - (-2) =$	$(12)(-2) =$	$\dfrac{12}{-2} =$
$(-4) + (-3) + (-2) =$	$(-4) - (-3) - (-2) =$	$(-4)(-3)(-2) =$	$\dfrac{(-4)(-3)}{(-2)} =$

Problem Solving Answer the question below.

Problem: How many cubic yards of concrete must be ordered to pour the section below?

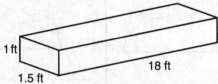

1 ft

1.5 ft

18 ft

Understand
What information am I given?
What am I asked to find or do?

Plan
How can I use the information I am given?
Which strategy should I try?

Solve
Did I follow the plan?
Did I show my work?
Did I write the answer?

Check
Did I use the correct information?
Did I do what was asked?
Is my answer reasonable?

Math Course 2

| **Facts** | Write the equivalent decimal and fraction for each percent. | | | | | |

Percent	Decimal	Fraction	Percent	Decimal	Fraction
10%			$33\frac{1}{3}\%$		
90%			20%		
5%			75%		
$12\frac{1}{2}\%$			$66\frac{2}{3}\%$		
50%			1%		
25%			250%		

| **Problem Solving** | Answer the question below. |

Problem: A goat is kept on a 4-meter chain connected to a metal hook in the ground. Approximately what area of grass can she eat? If she is chained at the center of the 8-m side of the garage what area of grass can she eat?

Understand
What information am I given?
What am I asked to find or do?

- -

Plan
How can I use the information I am given?
Which strategy should I try?

- -

Solve
Did I follow the plan?
Did I show my work?
Did I write the answer?

- -

Check
Did I use the correct information?
Did I do what was asked?
Is my answer reasonable?

Name _____ Time _____

Facts Find the area of each figure. Angles that look like right angles are right angles.

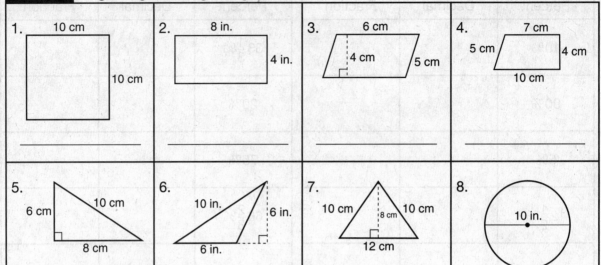

1. 10 cm / 10 cm

_____

2. 8 in. / 4 in.

_____

3. 6 cm / 4 cm / 5 cm

_____

4. 7 cm / 5 cm / 4 cm / 10 cm

_____

5. 6 cm / 10 cm / 8 cm

_____

6. 10 in. / 6 in. / 6 in.

_____

7. 10 cm / 8 cm / 10 cm / 12 cm

_____

8. 10 in.

Leave π as π.

_____

Problem Solving Answer the question below.

Problem: A summer baseball league is made up of four teams. If each team will play each other three times, how many games must be scheduled?

Understand
What information am I given?
What am I asked to find or do?

- -

Plan
How can I use the information I am given?
Which strategy should I try?

- -

Solve
Did I follow the plan?
Did I show my work?
Did I write the answer?

- -

Check
Did I use the correct information?
Did I do what was asked?
Is my answer reasonable?

 Saxon Math Course 2

Facts	Write each number in scientific notation.	
186,000 =	0.0005 =	30,500,000 =
2.5 billion =	12 million =	$\dfrac{1}{1,000,000}$ =

Write each number in standard form.

1×10^6 =	1×10^{-6} =	2.4×10^4 =
5×10^{-4} =	4.75×10^5 =	2.5×10^{-3} =

Problem Solving   Answer the question below.

Problem: Candis has an 11-liter can and a 5-liter can. How can she measure out exactly 7 liters of water into a third unmarked container?

Understand
What information am I given?
What am I asked to find or do?

- -

Plan
How can I use the information I am given?
Which strategy should I try?

- -

Solve
Did I follow the plan?
Did I show my work?
Did I write the answer?

- -

Check
Did I use the correct information?
Did I do what was asked?
Is my answer reasonable?

Facts Simplify.

$6 + 6 \times 6 - 6 \div 6 =$	$3^2 + \sqrt{4} + 5(6) - 7 + 8 =$
$4 + 2(3 + 5) - 6 \div 2 =$	$2 + 2[3 + 4(7 - 5)] =$
$\sqrt{1^3 + 2^3 + 3^3} =$	$\dfrac{4 + 3(7 - 5)}{6 - (5 - 4)} =$
$(-3)(-3) + (-3) - (-3) =$	$\dfrac{3(-3) - (-3)(-3)}{(-3) - (3)(-3)} =$

Problem Solving Answer the question below.

Problem: Some tiled floors use regular hexagonal tiles because the tiles can be arranged side-to-side and end-to-end without gaps or overlaps. What geometric properties determine whether a regular polygon can tile a floor the same way? Identify two other regular polygons with these properties. Can regular pentagons or octagons be used to tile a floor as described?

Understand
What information am I given?
What am I asked to find or do?

- -

Plan
How can I use the information I am given?
Which strategy should I try?

- -

Solve
Did I follow the plan?
Did I show my work?
Did I write the answer?

- -

Check
Did I use the correct information?
Did I do what was asked?
Is my answer reasonable?

Saxon Math Course 2

Name _____ Time _____

Facts	Complete each step to solve each equation.		
$2x + 5 = 45$ $2x =$ $x =$	$3y + 4 = 22$ $3y =$ $y =$	$5n - 3 = 12$ $5n =$ $n =$	$3m - 7 = 14$ $3m =$ $m =$
$15 = 3a - 6$ $= 3a$ $= a$	$24 = 2w + 6$ $= 2w$ $= w$	$-2x + 9 = 23$ $-2x =$ $x =$	$20 - 3y = 2$ $-3y =$ $y =$
$\frac{1}{2}m + 6 = 18$ $\frac{1}{2}m =$ $m =$	$\frac{3}{4}n - 12 = 12$ $\frac{3}{4}n =$ $n =$	$3y + 1.5 = 6$ $3y =$ $y =$	$0.5w - 1.5 = 4.5$ $0.5w =$ $w =$

Problem Solving   Answer the question below.

Problem: Sharon took her daughter Susan to a playground. Use the graph to write a brief story about what Susan was doing on the playground.

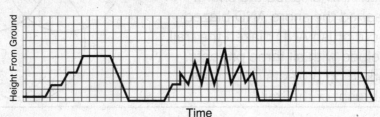

Understand

What information am I given?

What am I asked to find or do?

- -

Plan

How can I use the information I am given?

Which strategy should I try?

- -

Solve

Did I follow the plan?

Did I show my work?

Did I write the answer?

- -

Check

Did I use the correct information?

Did I do what was asked?

Is my answer reasonable?

Facts	Solve each equation.		
$6x + 2x =$	$6x - 2x =$	$(6x)(2x) =$	$\dfrac{6x}{2x} =$
$9xy + 3xy =$	$9xy - 3xy =$	$(9xy)(3xy) =$	$\dfrac{9xy}{3xy} =$
$x + y + x =$	$x + y - x =$	$(x)(y)(-x) =$	$\dfrac{xy}{x} =$
$3x + x + 3 =$	$3x - x - 3 =$	$(3x)(-x)(-3) =$	$\dfrac{(2x)(8xy)}{4y} =$

Problem Solving   Answer the question below.

Problem: 40 scouts went on a camping trip.
During 3-days, 14 scouts cleaned-up the
lakeshore, 13 cut down overgrown brush,
and 16 blazed a hiking trail. Three of these
scouts cut brush AND cleaned the shore.
Five scouts cleaned the shore AND blazed
the trail. Eight cut brush AND blazed the trail.
Two of them helped with all three projects.
How many worked on projects other than
the shore, the brush, or the trail?

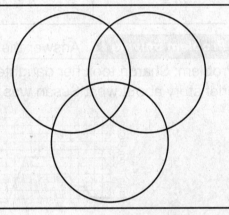

Understand
What information am I given?
What am I asked to find or do?

- -

Plan
How can I use the information I am given?
Which strategy should I try?

- -

Solve
Did I follow the plan?
Did I show my work?
Did I write the answer?

- -

Check
Did I use the correct information?
Did I do what was asked?
Is my answer reasonable?

Name _____ Time _____

Math Course 2

Facts   Simplify. Write each answer in scientific notation.

$(1 \times 10^6)(1 \times 10^6) =$	$(3 \times 10^3)(3 \times 10^3) =$	$(4 \times 10^{-5})(2 \times 10^{-6}) =$
$(5 \times 10^5)(5 \times 10^5) =$	$(6 \times 10^{-3})(7 \times 10^{-4}) =$	$(3 \times 10^6)(2 \times 10^{-4}) =$
$\dfrac{8 \times 10^8}{2 \times 10^2} =$	$\dfrac{5 \times 10^6}{2 \times 10^3} =$	$\dfrac{9 \times 10^3}{3 \times 10^8} =$
$\dfrac{2 \times 10^6}{4 \times 10^2} =$	$\dfrac{1 \times 10^{-3}}{4 \times 10^8} =$	$\dfrac{8 \times 10^{-8}}{2 \times 10^{-2}} =$

Problem Solving   Answer the question below.

Problem: A friend tells you, "The probability of 3 tossed coins turning up all heads or tails is $\frac{1}{2}$, because anytime you toss 3 coins, at least 2 must match (2 heads or 2 tails), so that means that the third coin determines the probability." Is your friend right? What do you think the probability is that 3 tossed coins will turn up all heads or all tails?

Understand
What information am I given?
What am I asked to find or do?

Plan
How can I use the information I am given?
Which strategy should I try?

Solve
Did I follow the plan?
Did I show my work?
Did I write the answer?

Check
Did I use the correct information?
Did I do what was asked?
Is my answer reasonable?

Page 42 Blank

Name _____

Score _____

1. When the product of 15 and 40 is
(1) divided by the sum of 15 and 45,
what is the quotient?

2. Use the numbers 4 and 5 to
(2) illustrate the Commutative Property
of Addition.

3. Justify the first two steps taken to
(2) simplify $4 \times 7 \times 5$.

$4 \times 7 \times 5$	given expression
$7 \times 4 \times 5$	**a.** _____
$7 \times (4 \times 5)$	**b.** _____
7×20	$4 \times 5 = 20$
140	$7 \times 20 = 140$

4. Use words to write 21600050.
(5)

5. Find the next three numbers in this
(4) sequence.

$$1, 4, 9, 16, \ldots$$

6. Write 75,000 in expanded notation.
(5)

7. Replace the circle with the proper
(4) comparison symbol.

$$-8 \bigcirc -11$$

8. If $a = 15$ and $b = 3$, then what
(1) does ab equal?

9. Use digits to write eight million, one
(5) hundred thousand, sixty.

Find each missing number for 10–15.

10. $x + \$4.30 = \$15.00$
(3)

11. $y - 8860 = 6300$
(3)

12. $8z = \$74.00$
(3)

13. $1426 - a = 78$
(3)

17. $1000 - (560 - 79)$
(2)

14. $45b = 1575$
(3)

18. $8\overline{)46,392}$
(1)

15. $32,800 - c = 9360$
(3)

19. $160(17)$
(1)

Simplify 16–20.

16. $18 \cdot 12 \cdot 11$
(1)

20. $\dfrac{\$29.50}{10}$
(1)

Saxon Math Course 2

Name _____

Score _____

1. When the product of 20 and 30 is
(1) divided by the sum of 20 and 30,
what is the quotient?

2. Use the numbers 5 and 6 to
(2) illustrate the Commutative Property
of Multiplication.

3. Justify the first two steps taken to
(2) simplify $6 \times 7 \times 5$.

$6 \times 7 \times 5$ given expression

$7 \times 6 \times 5$ **a.** _____

$7 \times (6 \times 5)$ **b.** _____

7×30 $6 \times 5 = 30$

210 $7 \times 30 = 210$

4. Use words to write 31020030.
(5)

5. Find the next three numbers in this
(4) sequence.

$$1, 4, 9, 16, 25, \ldots$$

6. Write 205,000 in expanded
(5) notation.

7. Replace the circle with the proper
(4) comparison symbol.

$$-9 \; \bigcirc \; -10$$

8. If $a = 12$ and $b = 4$, then what
(1) does ab equal?

9. Use digits to write twelve million,
(5) three hundred thousand, forty.

Find each missing number for 10–15.

10. $a + \$3.40 = \$15.00$
(3)

11. $b - 5630 = 7240$
(3)

12. $6c = \$42.60$
(3)

13. $3714 + e = 5860$
(3)

14. $35d = 770$
(3)

15. $3400 - f = 986$
(3)

Simplify 16–20.

16. $6 \cdot 12 \cdot 15$
(1)

17. $1000 - (650 - 97)$
(2)

18. $9)\overline{46,306}$
(1)

19. $150(16)$
(1)

20. $\dfrac{\$76.50}{10}$
(1)

Saxon Math Course

Name _____

Score _____

1. Three dimes is
(8)
   a. what fraction of a dollar?
   b. what percent of a dollar?

6. Use the numbers 2, 3, and 5 to
(2) illustrate the Associative Property
of Addition.

2. In this triangle, which segment is
(7) perpendicular to $\overline{AC}$?

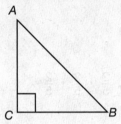

7.
(8)

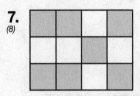

   a. What fraction of the rectangle is
shaded?

   b. What fraction of the rectangle is
not shaded?

3. How many $\frac{3}{4}$'s are in 1?
(9)

8. Subtract fifty-eight million from one
(5) hundred million, and use words to
write the difference.

4. Write $3\frac{1}{8}$ as an improper fraction.
(10)

5. a. Arrange these numbers in order
(4) from least to greatest:

$$\frac{1}{3}, -3, 3, 0$$

   b. Which of the numbers in part
a is not an integer?

9. a. List the factors of 21.
(6)
   b. List the factors of 48.

   c. Which numbers are factors of
both 21 and 48?

   d. What is the greatest common
factor of 21 and 48?

10. Which property of multiplication is
(9) illustrated by this equation?

$$\frac{3}{4} \times \frac{4}{3} = 1$$

16. $\frac{3}{5} \times \frac{4}{7}$
(9)

17. $9\overline{)74,309}$
(1)

Find each missing number for 11–13.

11. $2320 + m = 4760$
(3)

18. $40(\$1.63)$
(1)

12. $n - \$8.75 = \$9.55$
(3)

13. $35p = 910$
(3)

19. $\frac{2}{5} \cdot \frac{2}{5} \cdot \frac{2}{5}$
(9)

20. Describe each figure as a line, ray,
(7) or segment. Then use a symbol and
letters to name each figure.

Simplify 14–19.

14. $\frac{3}{5} + \frac{1}{5}$
(9)

a.

b.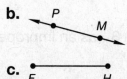

c.
$\underset{FH}{\bullet\!\!-\!\!-\!\!-\!\!-\!\!-\!\!-\!\!\bullet}$

15. $\frac{9}{11} - \frac{3}{11}$
(9)

Saxon Math Course 2

Name _____

Score _____

1. Seven dimes is
(8)
   a. what fraction of a dollar?
   b. what percent of a dollar?

2. In this triangle, which angle is not
(7) acute?

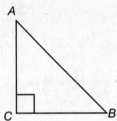

3. How many $\frac{2}{3}$'s are in 1?
(9)

4. Write $6\frac{2}{3}$ as an improper fraction.
(10)

5. a. Arrange these numbers in order
(4)   from least to greatest:

$$\frac{1}{2}, -2, 2, 0$$

   b. Which of the numbers in part
   a is not an integer?

6. Use the numbers 2, 3, and 6 to
(2) illustrate the Associative Property
of Multiplication.

7.
(8)

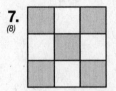

   a. What fraction of the square is
   shaded?
   b. What fraction of the square is
   not shaded?

8. Subtract forty-seven million from
(5) one hundred million, and use words
to write the difference.

9. a. List the factors of 27.
(6)   **b.** List the factors of 45.
   c. Which numbers are factors of
   both 27 and 45?
   d. What is the greatest common
   factor of 27 and 45?

10. Which property of multiplication is illustrated by this equation?
(9)

$$\frac{2}{3} \times \frac{3}{2} = 1$$

16. $\frac{2}{5} \times \frac{3}{7}$
(9)

17. $8)\overline{74,000}$
(1)

Find each missing number for 11–13.

11. $5370 + q = 6184$
(3)

18. $40(\$1.75)$
(1)

12. $r - \$7.85 = \$9.50$
(3)

19. $\frac{3}{4} \cdot \frac{1}{2} \cdot \frac{3}{5}$
(9)

13. $35t = 840$
(3)

20. Describe each figure as a line, ray
(7) or segment. Then use a symbol a
letters to name each figure.

Simplify 14–19.

14. $\frac{3}{7} + \frac{2}{7}$
(9)

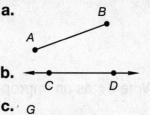

15. $\frac{8}{9} - \frac{4}{9}$
(9)

 Saxon Math Course 2

1. In 1990 Ashton's population was
(12)   96,212. By the 2000 census,
its population had increased to
100,219. Ashton's population in
2000 was how much greater than
its population in 1990?

2. The beach balls arrived packed
(13)   15 in each case. If 80 cases were
delivered, how many beach balls
were there in all?

3. The product of 7 and 9 is how
(1, 12)   much greater than the sum of
7 and 9?

4. Sam spent $8.75 for the ticket,
(11) $3.50 for popcorn, and 90¢ for a
drink. How much did he spend in
all?

5. How many years were there from
(12)   1673 to 1699?

6. If 28% of the students ride bikes
(14)   to school, what percent of the
students do not ride bikes to
school?

7. Draw and shade circles to show
(10)   that $3\frac{1}{3} = \frac{10}{3}$.

8. Complete each equivalent fraction.
(15)
   a. $\frac{3}{4} = \frac{?}{12}$

   b. $\frac{2}{3} = \frac{?}{12}$

9. Find a fraction equal to $\frac{2}{3}$ that has
(15)   a denominator of 6. Then subtract
that fraction from $\frac{5}{6}$. What is the
difference?

10. **a.** List the factors of 21.
(6)
   b. List the factors of 42.

   c. What is the greatest common
   factor of 21 and 42?

11. Name three segments in this figure
(7) in order of length from shortest to
longest.

12. What mixed number is represented
(8) by point *A* on this number line?

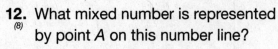

Simplify 13–18.

13. $\frac{7}{11} + \frac{5}{11}$
(10)

14. $\frac{2}{3} \cdot \frac{7}{4}$
(15)

15. $7\overline{)15,409}$
(1)

16. $\frac{8840}{40}$
(1)

17. $\begin{array}{r} 735 \\ \times\ 14 \\ \hline \end{array}$
(1)

18. $(9 + 4)(3)$
(2)

Find each missing number for 19–20.

19. $15x = 4500$
(3)

20. $\$20.00 - r = \$8.43$
(3)

Saxon Math Course 2

Score _____

1. In 1990 Deerfield's population
(12) was 27,312. By the 2000 census,
its population had increased to
31,080. Deerfield's population in
2000 was how much greater than
its population in 1990?

2. The beach balls arrived packed
(13) 18 in each case. If 50 cases were
delivered, how many beach balls
were there in all?

3. The product of 7 and 6 is how
(1, 12) much greater than the sum of
7 and 6?

4. Leticia spent $8.50 for the ticket,
(11) $2.75 for popcorn, and 90¢ for a
drink. How much did she spend in
all?

5. How many years were there from
(12) 1776 to 1789?

6. If 26% of the students ride the
(14) bus to school, what percent of the
students do not ride the bus to
school?

7. Draw and shade circles to show
(10) that $2\frac{1}{2} = \frac{5}{2}$.

8. Complete each equivalent fraction.
(16)
  a. $\frac{5}{6} = \frac{?}{12}$

  b. $\frac{1}{2} = \frac{?}{12}$

9. Find a fraction equal to $\frac{1}{2}$ that has
(15) a denominator of 8. Then subtract
that fraction from $\frac{7}{8}$. What is the
difference?

10. a. List the factors of 15.
(6)
  b. List the factors of 30.

  c. What is the greatest common
  factor of 15 and 30?

11. Name three segments in this figure
(7) in order of length from shortest to
longest.

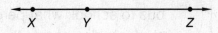

12. What mixed number is represented
(8) by point *B* on this number line?

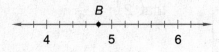

Simplify 13–18.

13. $\frac{5}{7} + \frac{3}{7}$
(10)

14. $\frac{3}{4} \cdot \frac{11}{6}$
(15)

15. $9\overline{)18,039}$
(1)

16. $\frac{8880}{30}$
(1)

17. $\begin{array}{r} 635 \\ \times\ 14 \\ \hline \end{array}$
(1)

18. $(6 + 5)(4)$
(2)

Find each missing number for 19–20.

19. $12t = 4500$
(3)

20. $\$20.00 - v = \$4.83$
(3)

Saxon Math Course 2

Name _____

Score _____

1. Great-Grandpa celebrated his
(12) seventy-fifth birthday in 2006. In
what year was he born?

2. The farmer harvested 8000 bushels
(13) of grain from 50 acres. The crop
produced an average of how many
bushels of grain for each acre?

3. One quart is what percent of one
(8, 16) gallon?

4. What is the probability the spinner
(14, 15) will stop on 2?

5. Forty-seven million is how much
(5, 12) less than one billion? Use words to
write the answer.

6. a. Compare:
(2, 9)

$$\left(\frac{1}{8} + \frac{3}{8}\right) + \frac{4}{8} \bigcirc \frac{1}{8} + \left(\frac{3}{8} + \frac{4}{8}\right)$$

b. What property is illustrated by
this comparison?

7. Use digits and symbols to write
(4) "Seven minus nine equals negative
two."

8.
(19, 20)

5 cm

9 cm

a. Find the perimeter of this
rectangle.

b. Find the area of this rectangle.

9. Reduce:
(15)

a. $3\frac{24}{36}$

b. $\frac{9}{21}$

Name _____

Score _____

1. Great-Grandma celebrated her
(12)   seventy-fifth birthday in 2007. In
       what year was she born?

2. The farmer harvested 7000 bushels
(13)   of grain from 50 acres. The crop
       produced an average of how many
       bushels of grain for each acre?

3. One foot is what percent of one
(8, 16) yard?

4. What is the probability the spinner
(14, 15) will stop on 2?

5. Seventy-four million is how much
(5, 12) less than one billion? Use words to
       write the answer.

6. a. Compare:
(2, 9)
$$\left(\frac{1}{6} + \frac{2}{6}\right) + \frac{3}{6} \bigcirc \frac{1}{6} + \left(\frac{2}{6} + \frac{3}{6}\right)$$

b. What property is illustrated by
       this comparison?

7. Use digits and symbols to write
(4)   "Seven minus ten equals negative
       three."

8.
(19, 20)

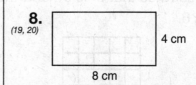

4 cm

8 cm

a. Find the perimeter of this
       rectangle.
b. Find the area of this rectangle.

9. Reduce:
(15)

a. $5\frac{18}{24}$

b. $\frac{12}{21}$

10. Write $1\frac{2}{3}$ as an improper fraction,
$_{(9,\,10)}$ and multiply the improper fraction
by $\frac{1}{2}$.

11. Complete each equivalent fraction.
$_{(15)}$

 a. $\frac{5}{6} = \frac{?}{36}$

 b. $\frac{5}{9} = \frac{?}{36}$

12. The square illustrates that 5^2 is 25
$_{(20)}$ and that $\sqrt{25}$ is 5. Draw a figure that
illustrates that 6^2 is 36 and that $\sqrt{36}$
is 6.

Find each missing number for 13–14.

13. $3797 - k = 1169$
$_{(3)}$

14. $30m = \$40.20$
$_{(3)}$

15. Which of the following does not
$_{(15)}$ equal $2\frac{1}{4}$?

 A. $\frac{9}{4}$

 B. $2\frac{2}{8}$

 C. $\frac{7}{4}$

 D. $\frac{18}{8}$

Simplify 16–20.

16. $\frac{3}{5} + \frac{3}{5} + \frac{3}{5}$
$_{(9)}$

17. $\frac{9}{10} - \frac{7}{10}$
$_{(9)}$

18. $\left(\frac{2}{3}\right)^2$
$_{(9,\,20)}$

19. $\sqrt{144}$
$_{(20)}$

20. $12(11 + 13)$
$_{(2)}$

Saxon Math Course

1. Six hundred twenty-four books
(13) were packed into 26 boxes. If each
box contained the same number
of books, how many books were
packed in each box?

2. The Holy Roman Empire lasted
(12) from 800 to 1806. How many years
did the Holy Roman Empire last?

3. Jan went to the ball game with
(11) $20.00 and returned with $9.30.
How much money did Jan spend at
the ball game?

4. Terrell was engrossed in his
(12) 340-page book. He stopped on
page 127 at noon to eat lunch. He
stopped on page 253 to eat dinner.
How many pages did Terrell read
between lunch and dinner?

5. Diagram this statement. Then
(22, 14) answer the questions that follow.

*Three eighths of the 64 marbles
in the bag were blue.*

a. How many marbles in the bag
were blue?

b. How many marbles in the bag
were not blue?

c. If one marble is drawn from the
bag, what is the probability of
drawing blue?

6. Use a compass and straightedge
(Inv. 2) to inscribe a regular hexagon in a
circle.

7. Write the prime factorization of 480.
(21)

8. Simplify:
(15)

a. $\dfrac{108}{8}$

b. $8\dfrac{8}{6}$

c. $\dfrac{120}{900}$

9. Which of these figures is a
(18)   polygon?

A.

B.

C.

D.

10. Complete each equivalent fraction.
(15)

a. $\frac{5}{8} = \frac{?}{48}$

b. $\frac{7}{16} = \frac{?}{48}$

Solve 11–13.

11. $350 = 700 - x$
(3)

12. $y - 48 = 25$
(3)

13. $12w = 264$
(3)

Simplify 14–19.

14. $7 - 1\frac{5}{6}$
(23)

15. $5\frac{4}{5} + 6\frac{3}{5}$
(10)

16. $5\frac{1}{8} - 1\frac{7}{8}$
(23)

17. $\frac{2}{3} \cdot \frac{3}{4} \cdot \frac{4}{5}$
(24)

18. $\frac{2}{3} \div \frac{1}{2}$
(25)

19. $10^2 - \sqrt{25}$
(20)

20. Refer to rectangle *ABCD* to answer
(7, 20)   questions **a** and **b**.

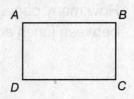

a. Which side of the rectangle is
      parallel to $\overline{BC}$?

b. If *AB* is 25 mm and *BC* is
      15 mm, what is the area of the
      rectangle?

Saxon Math Course 2

1. Six hundred twenty-four books
(13) were packed into 24 boxes. If each
box contained the same number
of books, how many books were
packed in each box?

2. How many years were there from
(12) 864 to 1509?

3. Nia went to the ball game with
(11) $20.00 and returned with $7.30.
How much money did Nia spend at
the ball game?

4. Tim was enjoying his 360-page
(12) book. He stopped on page 137 at
noon to eat lunch. He stopped on
page 223 to eat dinner. How many
pages did Tim read between lunch
and dinner?

5. Diagram this statement. Then
(22, 14) answer the questions that follow.

> *One fourth of the 64 marbles in*
> *the bag were red.*

a. How many marbles in the bag
were red?

b. How many marbles in the bag
were not red?

c. If one marble is drawn from the
bag, what is the probability of
drawing red?

6. Use a compass and straightedge
(Inv. 2) to inscribe a regular triangle in a
circle.

7. Write the prime factorization of 490.
(21)

8. Simplify:
(15)

   a. $\frac{66}{9}$

   b. $6\frac{6}{9}$

   c. $\frac{660}{900}$

9. Which of these figures is not a
(18) polygon?

A.

B.

C.

D.

10. Complete each equivalent fraction.
(15)

    a. $\dfrac{5}{8} = \dfrac{?}{24}$

    b. $\dfrac{5}{12} = \dfrac{?}{24}$

Solve 11–13.

11. $250 = 600 - x$
(3)

12. $y - 25 = 46$
(3)

13. $12w = 276$
(3)

Simplify 14–19.

14. $6 - 1\dfrac{1}{6}$
(23)

15. $5\dfrac{4}{5} + 3\dfrac{4}{5}$
(10)

16. $3\dfrac{1}{8} - 1\dfrac{3}{8}$
(23)

17. $\dfrac{2}{5} \cdot \dfrac{5}{6} \cdot \dfrac{6}{7}$
(24)

18. $\dfrac{2}{3} \div \dfrac{1}{4}$
(25)

19. $10^2 - \sqrt{100}$
(20)

20. Refer to rectangle *ABCD* to answe
(7, 20) questions **a** and **b**.

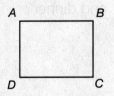

    a. Which side of the rectangle is
        parallel to $\overline{CD}$?

    b. If *AB* is 20 mm and *BC* is
        15 mm, what is the area of the
        rectangle?

 Saxon Math Course 2

Name _____

Score _____

1. The 5 starters on the basketball
(28) team were tall. Their heights were
70 inches, 71 inches, 72 inches,
73 inches, and 84 inches. What
was the average height of the
5 starters?

5. Diagram this statement. Then
(22) answer the questions that follow.

*The Daltons completed 20% of
their 2170-mile trip the first day.*

  a. How many miles did they travel
  the first day?

  b. How many miles of their trip did
  they still have to travel?

2. Marie bought 8 pounds of apples
(28) for $0.82 per pound and paid for
them with a ten-dollar bill. How
much should she get back in
change?

6. If the perimeter of a square is
(19) 3 feet, how many inches long is
each side of the square?

3. On the first day of their 2598-mile
(11) trip, the Kalsbeeks drove 683 miles.
How many more miles do they have
to drive until they complete their trip?

7. Rewrite $\frac{2}{5}$ and $\frac{3}{4}$ so that they have
(30) common denominators. Then add
the fractions and simplify the sum.

4. The coordinates of three vertices
(Inv. 3) of a square are (1, −1), (6, −1), and
(6, 4).

  a. What are the coordinates of the
  fourth vertex?

  b. What is the area of the square?

8. Describe the rule of this function.
(16)

Input	Output
1	4
2	8
3	12
4	16

9. Estimate the quotient when 29,376
(29) is divided by 29.

10. Reduce: $\frac{120}{540}$
(24)

11. Compare: $\frac{3}{5} \bigcirc \frac{5}{3}$
(30)

12. Find the least common multiple
(27) (LCM) of 8 and 12.

13. The figure shows a circle with the
(7, Inv. 2) center at *M*.

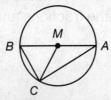

   a. Which chord is a diameter?

   b. Which inscribed angle appears
      to be a right angle?

14. a. Write the prime factorization of
(21)   225.

   b. Find $\sqrt{225}$.

Solve 15–17.

15. $7w = 4 \cdot 21$
(3)

16. $417 + a = 653$
(3)

17. $91 - d = 42$
(3)

Simplify 18–20.

18. $\frac{1}{4} + \frac{1}{3}$
(30)

19. $\left(\frac{3}{4} \cdot \frac{1}{3}\right) - \frac{1}{6}$
(30)

20. $1\frac{3}{5} \div 2\frac{1}{2}$
(26)

Saxon Math Course 2

1. The 5 starters on the basketball
(28) team were tall. Their heights were
71 inches, 72 inches, 73 inches,
75 inches, and 84 inches. What
was the average height of the
5 starters?

2. Miguel bought 7 pounds of apples
(28) for $0.78 per pound and paid
for them with a ten-dollar bill.
How much should he get back in
change?

3. On the first day of their 2058-mile
(11) trip, the Martins drove 586 miles.
How many more miles do they have
to drive until they complete their
trip?

4. The coordinates of three vertices
(Inv. 3) of a square are (1, −2), (5, −2), and
(5, 2).
   a. What are the coordinates of the
   fourth vertex?
   b. What is the area of the square?

5. Diagram this statement. Then
(22) answer the questions that follow.

   *The Claytons completed 20% of
   their 2030-mile trip the first day.*

   a. How many miles did they travel
   the first day?
   b. How many miles of their trip did
   they still have to travel?

6. If the perimeter of a square is
(19) 5 feet, how many inches long is
each side of the square?

7. Rewrite $\frac{3}{5}$ and $\frac{3}{4}$ so that they have
(30) common denominators. Then add
the fractions and simplify the sum.

8. Describe the rule of this function.
(16)

Input	Output
1	5
2	10
3	15
4	20

9. Estimate the quotient when 20,260
(29) is divided by 19.

10. Reduce: $\frac{120}{270}$
(24)

11. Compare: $\frac{3}{4}$ ◯ $\frac{4}{3}$
(30)

12. Find the least common multiple
(27) (LCM) of 10 and 12.

13. The figure shows a circle with the
(7, Inv. 2) center at M.

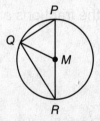

a. Which chord is a diameter?

b. Which central angle appears to
be an acute angle?

14. a. Write the prime factorization of
(21) 441.

b. Find $\sqrt{441}$.

Solve 15–17.

15. $7w = 5 \cdot 14$
(3)

16. $516 + m = 653$
(3)

17. $81 - f = 42$
(3)

Simplify 18–20.

18. $\frac{3}{4} - \frac{1}{3}$
(30)

19. $\left(\frac{3}{4} \cdot \frac{2}{3}\right) - \frac{1}{6}$
(30)

20. $2\frac{1}{2} \div 1\frac{3}{5}$
(26)

Saxon Math Course 2

10. Write $2\frac{1}{2}$ as an improper fraction,
(9, 10) and multiply the improper fraction
by $\frac{1}{3}$.

11. Complete each equivalent fraction.
(15)

  a. $\frac{3}{4} = \frac{?}{36}$

  b. $\frac{4}{9} = \frac{?}{36}$

12. The square illustrates 6^2 is 36 and
(20) that $\sqrt{36}$ is 6. Draw a figure that
illustrates that 5^2 is 25 and that $\sqrt{25}$
is 5.

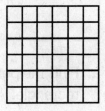

Find each missing number for 13–14.

13. $7937 - g = 1169$
(3)

14. $30y = \$41.10$
(3)

15. Which of the following does not
(15) equal $2\frac{2}{3}$?

  A. $\frac{11}{3}$

  B. $2\frac{4}{6}$

  C. $\frac{8}{3}$

  D. $2\frac{10}{15}$

Simplify 16–20.

16. $\frac{3}{4} + \frac{3}{4} + \frac{3}{4}$
(9)

17. $\frac{9}{11} - \frac{7}{11}$
(9)

18. $\left(\frac{3}{4}\right)^2$
(9, 20)

19. $\sqrt{121}$
(20)

20. $13(11 + 13)$
(2)

Saxon Math Course 2

Name _____

Score _____

1. In the first four months of the year
(28) the Montgomerys' electric bills
were $120.46, $134.59, $118.38,
and $96.29. What was the
Montgomerys' average electricity
bill during the first four months of
the year?

2. The price was reduced from four
(12) thousand, four hundred ninety-six
dollars to one thousand, eight
hundred ninety-three dollars. By
how much was the price reduced?

3. A one-year subscription to the
(28) monthly magazine costs $15.60.
The regular newsstand price is
$1.95 per issue. How much is
saved per issue by paying the
subscription price?

4. Jenna ran one lap in 65.2 seconds.
(12, 35) Gloria ran one lap in 62.7 seconds.
Gloria's time was how many
seconds less than Jenna's time?

5. The perimeter of the square
(19) equals the perimeter of the regular
pentagon. Each side of the
pentagon is 16 cm. How long is
each side of the square?

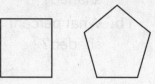

6. Diagram this statement. Then
(22) answer the questions that follow.

*Four ninths of the 63 fish in the
tank were guppies.*

a. How many of the fish were
guppies?

b. How many of the fish were not
guppies?

7. Find the least common multiple
(27) (LCM) of 7, 9, and 21.

8. Estimate the product of 3.14 and
(33) 5.125 by rounding each number to
the nearest whole number before
multiplying.

9.
(8)

a. What fraction of this square is shaded?

b. What percent of this square is shaded?

10. What decimal number is halfway between 14 and 15?
(34)

11. The coordinates of three vertices of a rectangle are (3, 2), (3, –3), and (–1, –3).
(Inv. 3)

a. What are the coordinates of the fourth vertex?

b. What is the area of the rectangle?

12. What decimal number names the point marked with an arrow on this number line?
(34)

13. Solve: $18x = 9 \cdot 10$
(3)

14. Use words to write 100.113.
(31)

Simplify 15–20.

15. 1.5×1.5
(35)

16. $6.25 \div 5$
(35)

17. $4.3 + 1.79 + 11$
(35)

18. $42.61 - 3.095$
(35)

19. $1\frac{1}{5} - \left(\frac{1}{4} \cdot \frac{2}{5}\right)$
(9, 30)

20. $\left(2\frac{1}{4} + 1\frac{1}{3}\right) \div \left(2 - 1\frac{1}{6}\right)$
(26, 30)

68

Saxon Math Course 2

1. In the first four months of the year
(28) the Gerardos' electric bills were
$115.46, $129.59, $113.38, and
$91.29. What was the Gerardos'
average electricity bill during the
first four months of the year?

2. The price was reduced from one
(12) thousand, two hundred ninety-six
dollars to nine hundred ninety-eight
dollars. By how much was the price
reduced?

3. A one-year subscription to the
(28) monthly magazine costs $14.88.
The regular newsstand price is
$1.95 per issue. How much is
saved per issue by paying the
subscription price?

4. Carla ran one lap in 62.8 seconds.
(12, 35) Ofelia ran one lap in 64.4 seconds.
Carla's lap was how many seconds
less than Ofelia's time?

5. The perimeter of the square
(19) equals the perimeter of the regular
pentagon. Each side of the square
is 15 cm. How long is each side of
the pentagon?

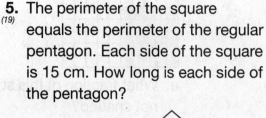
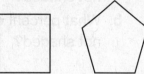

6. Diagram this statement. Then
(22) answer the questions that follow.

*Four sevenths of the 63 fish in
the tank were guppies.*

   a. How many of the fish were
   guppies?

   b. How many of the fish were not
   guppies?

7. Find the least common multiple
(27) (LCM) of 10, 12, and 15.

8. Estimate the product of 3.14 and
(33) 6.25 by rounding each number to
the nearest whole number before
multiplying.

9.
(8)

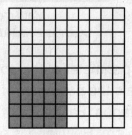

a. What fraction of this square is not shaded?

b. What percent of this square is not shaded?

10. What decimal number is halfway
(34) between 16 and 17?

11. The coordinates of three vertices
(Inv. 3) of a rectangle are (−1, 3), (2, 3), and
(2, −2).

a. What are the coordinates of the fourth vertex?

b. What is the area of the rectangle?

12. What decimal number names the
(34) point marked with an arrow on this
number line?

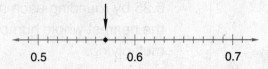

13. Solve: $16x = 8 \cdot 10$
(3)

14. Use words to write 100.13.
(31)

Simplify 15–20.

15. 1.2×1.2
(35)

16. $3.75 \div 5$
(35)

17. $3.4 + 1.78 + 12$
(35)

18. $21.62 - 3.083$
(35)

19. $1\frac{2}{5} - \left(\frac{3}{4} \cdot \frac{1}{5}\right)$
(9, 30)

20. $\left(2\frac{1}{4} - 1\frac{1}{3}\right) \div \left(2 + 1\frac{1}{6}\right)$
(26, 30)

Saxon Math Course 2

Name _____

Score _____

1. The bag contained only red
(36) marbles and white marbles. If
the ratio of red marbles to white
marbles was 5 to 4, what fraction of
the marbles were white?

Refer to the rectangle below for problems
5 and 6.

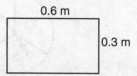

0.6 m

0.3 m

5. What is the perimeter of this
(35) polygon?

2. John ran 4 laps of the track in
(28) 5 minutes 40 seconds.

  a. How many seconds did it take
    John to run 4 laps?

  b. What was the average number
    of seconds it took John to run
    each lap?

6. What is the area of this polygon?
(35)

7. *AB* is 35 mm. *CD* is 45 mm. *AD* is
(7) 110 mm. Find *BC*.

A   B   C   D

3. Claire's car averages 21 miles per
(46) gallon of gas. At that rate, how far
would it go on 21 gallons?

8. The length of segment *CD* in
(32) problem 7 is 45 mm. What is
the length of segment *CD* in
centimeters?

4. Diagram this statement. Then
(22) answer the questions that follow.

   *Seventy-five percent of the
   104 adults in the McGlaughlin
   clan were 5 feet tall or taller.*

  a. How many of the adults were
    less than 5 feet tall?

  b. How many of the adults were
    5 feet tall or taller?

9. A coin is tossed and the spinner
(36) is spun. One possible outcome is
H3 (heads, 3). What is the sample
space for the experiment?

Simplify 14–18.

14. 0.12(0.06)
(35)

15. 0.144 ÷ 6
(35)

16. $5\frac{1}{3} - 3\frac{5}{6}$
(23)

10. If two angles of a triangle each
(40) measure 50°, then what is the
measure of the third angle of the
triangle?

17. $8\frac{1}{4} \cdot 1\frac{7}{11}$
(26)

11. What decimal number names point
(34) C on this number line?

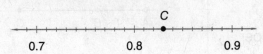

18. $5\frac{4}{9} \div 7$
(26)

12. Write sixty-five and three
(31) hundredths
a. as a decimal number
b. as a mixed number.

Solve 19–20.

19. $\frac{8}{10} = \frac{w}{15}$
(39)

20. $m + 0.72 = 1.54$
(3, 35)

13. What is the area of this triangle?
(37)

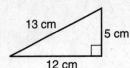

Saxon Math Course 2

Name _____

Score _____

1. The bag contained only red
(36) marbles and blue marbles. If the
ratio of red marbles to blue marbles
was 5 to 3, what fraction of the
marbles were blue?

2. James ran 4 laps of the track in
(28) 6 minutes 20 seconds.

   a. How many seconds did it take
James to run 4 laps?

   b. What was the average number
of seconds it took James to run
each lap?

3. Maria's car averages 24 miles per
(46) gallon of gas. At that rate, how far
would it go on 18 gallons?

4. Diagram this statement. Then
(22) answer the questions that follow.

   *Eighty percent of the 105 adults
in the McCoy clan were 5 feet tall
or taller.*

   a. How many of the adults were
less than 5 feet tall?

   b. How many of the adults were
5 feet tall or taller?

Refer to the rectangle below for problems
5 and 6.

0.8 m

0.4

5. What is the perimeter of this
(35) polygon?

6. What is the area of this polygon?
(35)

7. *AB* is 25 mm. *CD* is 45 mm. *AD* is
(7) 110 mm. Find *BC*.

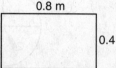

    A   *B*   *C*   *D*

8. The length of segment *AB* in
(32) problem 7 is 25 mm. What is
the length of segment *AB* in
centimeters?

9. A coin is tossed and the spinner
(36) is spun. One possible outcome is
      H2 (heads, 2). What is the sample
      space for the experiment?

Simplify 14–18.

14. 0.15(0.05)
(35)

15. 0.144 ÷ 8
(35)

16. $5\frac{2}{3} - 2\frac{5}{6}$
(23)

10. If two angles of a triangle each
(40) measure 70°, then what is the
      measure of the third angle of the
      triangle?

17. $6\frac{1}{4} \cdot 1\frac{3}{5}$
(26)

11. What decimal number names point
(34) C on this number line?

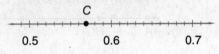

18. $7 \div 5\frac{4}{9}$
(26)

12. Write thirty-four and seven
(31) hundredths
   a. as a decimal number
   b. as a mixed number.

Solve 19–20.

19. $\frac{6}{10} = \frac{w}{15}$
(39)

20. $m + 0.27 = 1.54$
(3, 35)

13. What is the area of this triangle?
(37)

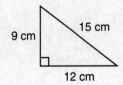

Name _____

Score _____

Cumulative Test **9A**

Math Course 2
Also take **Power-Up Test 9**

1. What is the probability of rolling
(36)   a prime number with one roll of a
       die?

2. Amber's test scores were 90, 91,
(28,   90, 87, 88, 95, 89, 80, 100, and
Inv. 4) 100.
   a. Find the mean of her scores.
   b. Find the median of her scores.

3. Evaluate: $a(b + c)$ if $a = 0.4$,
(41) $b = 2.1$, and $c = 0.4$

4. Refer to this election tally sheet to
(38)   answer questions **a** and **b**.

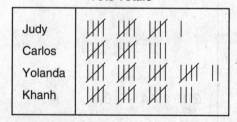

Vote Totals

Judy														
Carlos														
Yolanda																			
Khanh																

   a. The second-place candidate
       received how many more votes
       than the third-place candidate?
   b. What fraction of the votes did
       Yolanda receive?

5. Find the area of a triangle whose
(Inv. 3, vertices have the coordinates
37)   (–1, 1), (–1, 5), and (4, 1).

6. Read this statement. Then answer
(22, 36) the questions that follow.

   *Three eighths of those who
   rode the Giant Gyro at the fair
   were euphoric. All the rest were
   vertiginous.*

   a. What fraction of those who rode
       the ride were vertiginous?
   b. What was the ratio of euphoric
       to vertiginous riders?

7. The perimeter of the rectangle is
(19)   68 cm. What is the length of the
       rectangle?

12 cm

Saxon Math Course 2   © Harcourt Achieve Inc. and Stephen Hake. All rights reserved.   **75**

8. Find m∠a, m∠b, and m∠c in this figure.
(40)

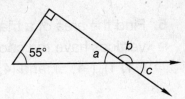

9. Write 225% as a decimal number.
(43)

10. Write $\frac{9}{5}$ as a decimal number.
(43)

11. Round $52.\overline{23}$ to three decimal places.
(42)

12. Divide 4.3 by 9 and write the quotient with a bar over the repetend.
(42)

Solve 13–15.

13. $\frac{12}{8} = \frac{0.3}{m}$
(39)

14. $7 = 3.14 + x$
(3, 35)

15. $0.091 = 1 - z$
(3, 35)

Simplify 16–20.

16. $5\frac{3}{5} + \frac{3}{4} + 2\frac{1}{2}$
(30)

17. $3\frac{1}{4} - \left(3 - 1\frac{5}{6}\right)$
(23)

18. $3\frac{3}{4} \cdot 3\frac{1}{5} \cdot 6$
(26)

19. $4 \div 10\frac{2}{3}$
(26)

20. $1.44 \div 0.6$
(35)

Saxon Math Course 2

1. What is the probability of rolling a
(36) composite number with one roll of
a die?

2. Eric's test scores were 90, 88, 88,
(28, 87, 84, 95, 90, 80, 98, and 100.
Inv. 4)
   a. Find the mean of his scores.

   b. Find the median of his scores.

3. Evaluate: $a(b + c)$ if $a = 0.2$,
(41) $b = 1.5$, and $c = 1$

4. Refer to this election tally sheet to
(38) answer questions **a** and **b**.

Vote Totals

Judy	𝍸𝍸 𝍸𝍸 𝍸𝍸 𝍸
Carlos	𝍸𝍸 𝍸𝍸 𝍸𝍸
Yolanda	𝍸𝍸 𝍸𝍸 𝍸𝍸 𝍸𝍸 𝍸𝍸
Khanh	𝍸𝍸 𝍸𝍸 𝍸𝍸 𝍸𝍸

   a. The first-place candidate
   received how many more votes
   than the third-place candidate?

   b. What fraction of the votes did
   Carlos receive?

5. Find the area of a triangle whose
(Inv. 3, vertices have the coordinates
37) (−1, −1), (−1, 3), and (5, −1).

6. Diagram this statement. Then
(22, 36) answer the questions that follow.

   *Four ninths of those who rode
   the Giant Gyro at the fair were
   euphoric. All the rest were
   vertiginous.*

   a. What fraction of those who rode
   the ride were vertiginous?

   b. What was the ratio of euphoric
   to vertiginous riders?

7. The perimeter of the rectangle is
(19) 60 cm. What is the length of the
rectangle?

12 cm

8. Find m∠a, m∠b, and m∠c in this figure.
(40)

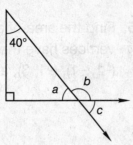

9. Write 125% as a decimal number.
(43)

10. Write $\frac{8}{5}$ as a decimal number.
(43)

11. Round $15.\overline{54}$ to three decimal places.
(42)

12. Divide 3.4 by 9 and write the quotient with a bar over the repetend.
(42)

Solve 13–15.

13. $\frac{12}{9} = \frac{0.8}{m}$
(39)

14. $6 = 3.14 + y$
(3, 35)

15. $0.91 = 1 - x$
(3, 35)

Simplify 16–20.

16. $5\frac{2}{5} + \frac{3}{4} + 3\frac{1}{2}$
(30)

17. $5\frac{1}{4} - \left(3 - 1\frac{1}{6}\right)$
(23)

18. $3\frac{3}{4} \cdot 3\frac{3}{5} \cdot 6$
(26)

19. $10\frac{2}{3} \div 4$
(26)

20. $1.44 \div 0.8$
(35)

Saxon Math Course

1. How far will a freight train travel
(46) in 3 hours at an average speed of
48 miles per hour?

2. Brand X costs $1.56 for 12 ounces.
(28) Brand Y costs 2¢ more per ounce.
What is the cost of 15 ounces of
Brand Y?

3. The ratio of black beans to sweet
(36) peas in the garden was 12 to 5.
What was the ratio of sweet peas
to black beans?

4. During the month of February,
(28) Hannah's weekly grocery bills were
$109.60, $114.56, $85.90, and
$122.14. Find Hannah's average
weekly grocery bill in February to
the nearest dollar.

5. Find the probability that the spinner
(14, 43) will stop on an even number.
Write the probability as a decimal
number.

6. Diagram this statement. Then
(22) answer the questions that follow.

*Forty percent of the 70 buttons in
the box had 5 holes.*

a. What fraction of the buttons did
not have 5 holes?

b. How many buttons did not have
5 holes?

7. Find the area of this figure.
(37)

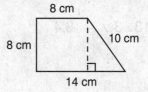

8. Write 24% as a reduced fraction.
(43)

9. Divide 4.8 by 11 and write the
(42) answer with a bar over the
repetend.

10. Reduce: $\frac{490}{560}$
(15)

11. If the perimeter of a square is
(19, 20) 32 inches, what is its area?

Solve 12–14.

12. $\frac{49}{56} = \frac{21}{f}$
(39)

13. $3w = 8.4$
(3, 35)

14. $5 - m = 1.36$
(3, 35)

Simplify 15–20.

15. $8^2 - 3^3$
(20)

16. 1 yd 2 ft 7 in.
(49) $+$ 2 yd 1 ft 8 in.

17. $14\frac{11}{12} - 8\frac{3}{8}$
(30)

18. $5\frac{3}{7} \div 3\frac{4}{5}$
(26)

19. 0.245×10^3
(47)

20. $0.1004 \div 0.08$
(45)

Saxon Math Course 2

Name _____

Score _____

1. How far will an 18-wheeler travel
(46) in 3 hours at an average speed of
54 miles per hour?

2. Brand X costs $1.65 for 11 ounces.
(28) Brand Y costs 2¢ more per ounce.
What is the cost of 15 ounces of
Brand Y?

3. The ratio of green beans to
(36) radishes in the garden was 5 to 2.
What was the ratio of radishes to
green beans?

4. During the month of February,
(28) George's weekly grocery bills were
$107.60, $112.56, $83.90, and
$120.14. Find George's average
weekly grocery bill in February to
the nearest dollar.

5. Find the probability that the spinner
(14, 43) will stop on an odd number.
Write the probability as a decimal
number.

6. Diagram this statement. Then
(22) answer the questions that follow.

*Thirty percent of the 70 buttons
had 4 holes.*

a. What fraction of the buttons did
not have 4 holes?

b. How many buttons did not have
4 holes?

7. Find the area of this figure.
(37)

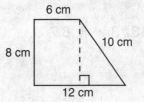

8. Write 28% as a reduced fraction.
(43)

9. Divide 4.9 by 11 and write the answer with a bar over the repetend.
(42)

10. Reduce: $\frac{560}{720}$
(15)

11. If the perimeter of a square is 28 inches, what is its area?
(19, 20)

Solve 12–14.

12. $\frac{35}{55} = \frac{21}{f}$
(39)

13. $3w = 8.7$
(3, 35)

14. $5 - n = 1.42$
(3, 35)

Simplify 15–20.

15. $8^2 - 4^3$
(20)

16.   2 yd 1 ft 9 in.
(49) $+$ 1 yd 2 ft 7 in.

17. $12\frac{5}{8} - 8\frac{7}{12}$
(30)

18. $5\frac{1}{5} \div 2\frac{1}{6}$
(26)

19. 0.425×10^3
(47)

20. $1.008 \div 0.08$
(45)

1. The ratio of schooners to skiffs in
(53) the bay was 7 to 5. If there were
63 schooners in the bay, how many
skiffs were there?

2. The average of four numbers is 98.
(55) If three of the numbers are 86, 87,
and 91, what is the fourth number?

3. A quart of milk costs 73¢. A case of
(28) 12 quarts costs $7.68. How much
is saved per quart by buying the
milk by the case?

4. Segment *AB* is how much longer
(8) than segment *BC*?

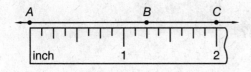

5. Diagram this statement. Then
(22) answer the questions that follow.

*Three tenths of the 40 vehicles
were trucks.*

   a. How many vehicles were
   trucks?

   b. What percent of the vehicles
   were trucks?

6. a. Write forty billion in scientific
(51)   notation.

   b. Write 1.86×10^7 in standard
   form.

7. Compare: $1.42 + 0.5 \bigcirc 5 - 3.09$
(33, 35)

8. Use a unit multiplier to convert
(50) 800 mm to cm.

9. Complete this table.
(48)

Fraction	Decimal	Percent
a.	b.	250%
$\frac{9}{10}$	c.	d.

14. $\frac{a}{8} = \frac{45}{10}$
(39)

10. Evaluate: $ab - bc$ if $a = 4$,
(52) $b = 3$, and $c = 2$

Simplify 15–20.

15. $13^2 - 2^5 - 3^3 - \sqrt{169}$
(20)

16. $4 + 4 \cdot 4 - 4 \div 4$
(52)

Refer to the figure below for problems
11 and 12. Dimensions are in inches. All
angles are right angles.

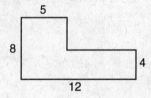

11. What is the area of the figure?
(37)

17. $2\frac{1}{4} + 2\frac{5}{6} + 3\frac{5}{8}$
(30)

18. $6\frac{2}{3} \cdot 5\frac{1}{4} \cdot 2\frac{1}{10}$
(26)

19. $0.4(0.25)(0.01)$
(35)

12. What is the perimeter of the figure?
(19)

20. $4.8 \div 0.016$
(45)

Solve 13–14.

13. $5.64 + w = 10$
(3, 35)

84

Saxon Math Course

1. The ratio of sailboats to dinghies
(53) in the bay was 5 to 7. If there were
70 sailboats in the bay, how many
dinghies were there?

2. The average of four numbers is 97.
(55) If three of the numbers are 87, 91,
and 99, what is the fourth number?

3. A liter of milk costs 68¢. A case of
(28) 12 liters costs $7.56. How much is
saved per liter by buying the milk
by the case?

4. Segment *AB* is how much longer
(8) than segment *BC*?

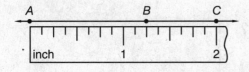

5. Read this statement. Then answer
(22) the questions that follow.

   Two fifths of the 40 vehicles were
   trucks.

   a. How many vehicles were
   trucks?

   b. What percent of the vehicles
   were trucks?

6. a. Write fourteen billion in scientific
(51) notation.

   b. Write 1.5×10^6 in standard
   form.

7. Compare: $3 - 1.08 \bigcirc 1.32 + 0.5$
(33, 35)

8. Use a unit multiplier to convert
(50) 600 mm to cm.

9. Complete this table.
(48)

Fraction	Decimal	Percent
a.	**b.**	350%
$\frac{7}{10}$	**c.**	**d.**

10. Evaluate: $ab - bc$ if $a = 5$, $b = 4$,
(52) and $c = 2$

Refer to the figure below for problems
11 and 12. Dimensions are in centimeters.
All angles are right angles.

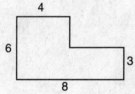

11. What is the area of the figure?
(37)

12. What is the perimeter of the figure?
(19)

Solve 13–14.

13. $6.54 + w = 10$
(3, 35)

14. $\frac{9}{a} = \frac{45}{10}$
(39)

Simplify 15–20.

15. $12^2 - 3^4 - 2^3 - \sqrt{144}$
(20)

16. $3 + 3 \cdot 3 - 3 \div 3$
(52)

17. $2\frac{3}{4} + 2\frac{1}{6} + 3\frac{7}{8}$
(30)

18. $5\frac{1}{3} \cdot 5\frac{1}{4} \cdot 1\frac{3}{4}$
(26)

19. $0.8(0.25)(0.05)$
(35)

20. $4.5 \div 0.015$
(45)

Saxon Math Course 2

Name _____

Score _____

1. If a half gallon of milk costs $1.24,
(16) what is the cost per pint?

2. The cookie recipe called for
(53) oatmeal and raisins in the ratio of
3 to 1. If 4 cups of oatmeal were
called for, how many cups of raisins
were needed?

3. Luzia ran the 400-meter race
(55) 3 times. Her fastest time was
52.3 seconds. Her slowest time
was 56.3 seconds. If Luzia's
average time was 54.0 seconds,
what was her time for the third
race?

4. The equation $y = 2x + 1$ is a
(41, 56) function rule. Copy and complete
this table by finding the values of
y for the given values of x.

x	y
0	
1	
2	
3	

5. What is the total cost of a $12.50
(60) item plus 6% sales tax?

6. Read this statement. Then answer
(22, 36) the questions that follow.

*Only four tenths of the print area
of the newspaper carried news.
The rest of the area was filled
with advertisements.*

a. What percent of the print area
was filled with advertisements?

b. What was the ratio of news area
to advertisement area?

7. a. Write 0.00205 in scientific
(57) notation.

b. Write 5.62×10^{-5} in standard
form.

8. Sketch a quadrilateral with only one
(Inv. 6) pair of parallel sides. What is this
type of quadrilateral called?

9. Use a unit multiplier to convert
(50) 1760 yards to feet.

10. Complete this table.
(48)

Fraction	Decimal	Percent
a.	**b.**	12%
$\frac{1}{25}$	**c.**	**d.**

Refer to the figure below for problems 11 and 12. Dimensions are in centimeters. All angles are right angles.

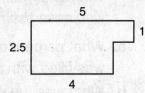

11. What is the perimeter of the figure?
(19)

12. What is the area of the figure?
(37)

Solve 13–14.

13. $\frac{4}{18} = \frac{n}{27}$
(39)

14. $p + 4.2 = 5$
(3, 35)

Simplify 15–20.

15. $10 + 10 \times 10 - 10 \div 10$
(52)

16. $10^4 - \sqrt{121} + 3^3 + 4^0$
(20)

17. $|{-12}|$
(59)

18. $5\frac{7}{9} + \left(2\frac{1}{3} - 1\frac{1}{2}\right)$
(30)

19. $7\frac{1}{2} \div \left(2\frac{2}{5} \div 4\right)$
(26)

20. $4.3(0.05)(0.005)$
(35)

Saxon Math Course 2

1. If a half gallon of milk costs $1.28,
(16) what is the cost per pint?

2. The cookie recipe called for raisins
(53) and nuts in the ratio of 3 to 2. If
1 cup of nuts was called for, how
many cups of raisins were needed?

3. Layla ran the 200-meter race
(55) 3 times. Her fastest time was
26.3 seconds. Her slowest time
was 30.3 seconds. If Layla's
average time was 28.0 seconds,
what was her time for the third
race?

4. The equation $y = 3x + 1$ is a
(41, 56) function rule. Copy and complete
this table by finding the values of
y for the given values of x.

x	y
0	
1	
2	
3	

5. What is the total cost of a $12.50
(60) item plus 8% sales tax?

6. Read this statement. Then answer
(22, 36) the questions that follow.

*Only three tenths of the print area
of the newspaper carried news.
The rest of the area was filled
with advertisements.*

a. What percent of the print area
was filled with advertisements?

b. What was the ratio of news area
to advertisement area?

7. a. Write 0.00405 in scientific
(57) notation.

b. Write 6.25×10^{-5} in standard
form.

8. Sketch a quadrilateral with two
(Inv. 6) pairs of parallel sides. What is the
name of this type of quadrilateral?

9. Use a unit multiplier to convert
(50) 1320 yards to feet.

10. Complete this table.
(48)

Fraction	Decimal	Percent
a.	b.	16%
$\frac{1}{20}$	c.	d.

Refer to the figure below for problems 11 and 12. Dimensions are in inches. All angles are right angles.

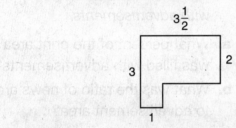

11. What is the perimeter of the figure?
(19)

12. What is the area of the figure?
(37)

Solve 13–14.

13. $\frac{10}{18} = \frac{n}{27}$
(39)

14. $p + 4.1 = 6$
(3, 35)

Simplify 15–20.

15. $5 + 5 \times 5 - 5 \div 5$
(52)

16. $10^3 - \sqrt{169} + 2^4 + 3^0$
(20)

17. $|-8|$
(59)

18. $5\frac{4}{9} + \left(3\frac{1}{2} - 1\frac{2}{3}\right)$
(30)

19. $3\frac{3}{4} \div \left(4 \div 2\frac{2}{5}\right)$
(26)

20. $2.2(0.05)(0.005)$
(35)

Saxon Math Course

Name _____

Score _____

1. What is the total price of a $10,000
(60) car plus 7.5% sales tax?

2. Emma worked for 7 hours and
(46) earned $38.50. How much did she
earn per hour?

3. The ratio of boys to girls in the
(53, 66) assembly was 5 to 4. If 180
students were in the assembly, how
many girls were there?

4. What is the average of $4\frac{1}{2}$, $3\frac{1}{3}$, 2,
(28, 30) and $2\frac{1}{6}$?

5. What number is 25% of 96?
(60)

6. Diagram this statement. Then
(22, 48) answer the questions that follow.

*Joel gave one fourth of his 236
postage stamps to his sister.*

  a. What percent of his postage
stamps did Joel give to his
sister?

  b. How many postage stamps did
Joel have left?

7. a. Write 0.00008 in scientific
(57) notation.

  b. Write 2.4×10^{-4} in standard
form.

8. In parallelogram *ABCD*, m∠*A* is
(61) 70°. Find m∠*B*.

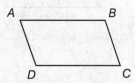

9. Compare: 4.5 km ◯ 4500 m
(32)

10. Divide 7 by 0.27 and write the
(33, 45) answer rounded to the nearest
whole number.

11. Find the sum:
(64) $(+6) + (-11) + (+5) + (-7)$

12. Complete this table.
(48)

Fraction	Decimal	Percent
$\frac{1}{5}$	a.	b.
c.	0.12	d.

13. Find the area of this parallelogram.
(61)

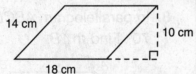

14 cm · 10 cm · 18 cm

14. Evaluate: $ab + a + b$
(52) if $a = \frac{1}{2}$ and $b = \frac{1}{4}$

Solve 15–16.

15. $\frac{w}{45} = \frac{8}{20}$
(39)

16. $2.5c = 0.125$
(3, 45)

Simplify 17–20.

17. $100 - 3[2(7 - 2)]$
(52, 63)

18. $4\frac{1}{4} + \left(2\frac{1}{6} - 1\frac{1}{3}\right)$
(30)

19. $5\frac{1}{4}\left(4 \div 1\frac{1}{2}\right)$
(26)

20. $0.5(0.1)(1.2)$
(35)

92   *Saxon Math* Course 2

Name _____

Score _____

1. What is the total price of a $10,000
(60) car plus 6.5% sales tax?

6. Diagram this statement. Then
(22, 48) answer the questions that follow.

*David gave one fifth of his 235
baseball cards to his sister.*

a. What percent of his baseball
cards did David give to his
sister?

b. How many baseball cards did
David have left?

2. Julie worked for 6 hours and
(46) earned $39.00. How much did she
earn per hour?

3. The ratio of girls to boys in the
(53, 66) assembly was 5 to 3. If 60 boys
were in the assembly, how many
girls were there?

7. a. Write 0.0006 in scientific
(57) notation.

b. Write 7.5×10^{-3} in standard
form.

4. What is the average of $5\frac{1}{2}$, 3, $4\frac{1}{3}$,
(28, 30) and $3\frac{1}{6}$?

8. In parallelogram $ABCD$, $m\angle A$ is
(61) 120°. Find $m\angle B$.

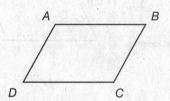

5. What number is 6% of 850?
(60)

9. Compare: 1.5 kg ◯ 150 g
(32)

10. Divide 8 by 0.15 and write the
(33, 45) answer rounded to the nearest
whole number.

11. Find the sum:
(64) $(-3) + (+3) + (-8) + (+12)$

12. Complete this table.
(48)

Fraction	Decimal	Percent
$\frac{4}{5}$	a.	b.
c.	0.15	d.

13. Find the area of this parallelogram.
(61)

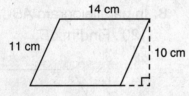

14 cm

11 cm 10 cm

14. Evaluate: $ab + a + b$
(52) if $a = \frac{1}{4}$ and $b = \frac{1}{2}$

Solve 15–16.

15. $\frac{w}{45} = \frac{12}{20}$
(39)

16. $1.5m = 2.25$
(3, 45)

Simplify 17–20.

17. $100 - 4[2(6 - 2)]$
(52, 63)

18. $3\frac{3}{4} + \left(2\frac{1}{6} - 1\frac{1}{3}\right)$
(30)

19. $7\frac{7}{8}\left(6 \div 2\frac{1}{4}\right)$
(26)

20. $0.05(0.1)(2.4)$
(35)

 Saxon Math Course 2

1. Pedro raced 96 kilometers from
(46) Perry to Medford and then idled
back. If the round trip took 8 hours,
what was Pedro's average speed in
kilometers per hour?

2. The ratio of dogs to cats in the
(66) neighborhood was 3 to 7. If a total
of 210 dogs and cats were in the
neighborhood, how many cats were
there?

3. Using a tape measure, Becky Jo
(65) found that the circumference of the
great redwood was 900 cm. She
estimated that its diameter was
300 cm. Was her estimate a little
too large or a little too small? Why?

4. Pistachios were priced at 3 pounds
(54) for $6.99.
a. What was the price per pound?
b. How much would 10 pounds of
pistachios cost?

5. If the product of six tenths and
(35) three tenths is subtracted from the
sum of two tenths and four tenths,
what is the difference?

6. Diagram this statement. Then
(22, 48) answer the questions that follow.

Three fifths of the baker's 60
cookies were chocolate cookies.

a. How many of the baker's
cookies were chocolate?
b. What percent of the baker's
cookies were not chocolate?

7. a. A cube has how many vertices?
(67, 70) **b.** What is the volume of this cube?

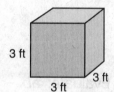

3 ft
3 ft
3 ft

8. Find the circumference of each
(65) circle.

11 cm

280 mm

a. Leave π as π.   **b.** Use $\frac{22}{7}$ for π.

9. Write each of these numbers in
(69) scientific notation:

   a. 11×10^{-7}

   b. 11×10^{7}

Refer to the figure below for problems
10 and 11. Dimensions are in millimeters.

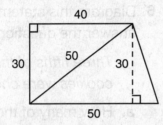

10. What is the area of the right
(37, 62) triangle?

11. What is the area of the isosceles
(37, 62) triangle?

12. Evaluate: $ab - (a - b)$
(52) if $a = 0.5$ and $b = 0.4$

13. What number is 25% of 1200?
(60)

14. Complete this table.
(48)

Fraction	Decimal	Percent
$\frac{1}{8}$	a.	b.
c.	d.	18%

15. Use a unit multiplier to convert
(50) 8000 g to kg.

Solve 16–17.

16. $q + 36 = 42.6$
(Inv. 7)

17. $5n = 32$
(Inv. 7)

Simplify 18–20.

18. $8.6 \times 5\frac{1}{4}$ (decimal answer)
(35, 43)

19. $(-6) + (-3) - (-1) - (+4)$
(68)

20. $1\frac{1}{3} \div \left(3\frac{1}{2} \cdot 2\right)$
(26)

Saxon Math Course

Name _____

Score _____

1. Malcomb coasted 32 miles from
(46) Moonridge to Mentone and then
pedaled back hard. If the round trip
took 4 hours, what was Malcomb's
average speed in miles per hour?

2. The ratio of dogs to cats in the
(66) neighborhood was 2 to 3. If a total
of 30 dogs and cats were in the
neighborhood, how many cats were
there?

3. Using a tape measure, Melanie
(65) found that the circumference of the
great redwood was 600 cm. She
estimated that its diameter was
200 cm. Was Melanie's estimate a
little too large or a little too small?
Why?

4. Parsnips were priced at 3 pounds
(54) for $1.23.
   a. What was the price per pound?
   b. How much would 10 pounds of
   parsnips cost?

5. If the product of four tenths and six
(35) tenths is subtracted from the sum
of four tenths and six tenths, what
is the difference?

6. Diagram this statement. Then
(22, 48) answer the questions that follow.

   *Two fifths of the baker's 60
   cookies were oatmeal.*

   a. How many of the baker's
   cookies were oatmeal?
   b. What percent of the baker's
   cookies were not oatmeal?

7. a. A cube has how many edges?
(67, 70) **b.** What is the volume of this cube?

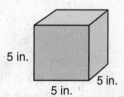

5 in.
5 in.
5 in.

8. Find the circumference of each
(65) circle.

8 in.
0.5 cm

   a. Leave π as π.   **b.** Use 3.14 for π.

9. Write each of these numbers in
(69)   scientific notation:

    a. 12×10^{-6}

    b. 12×10^{6}

Refer to the figure below for problems
10 and 11. Dimensions are in millimeters.

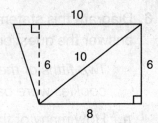

10. What is the area of the right
(37, 62)   triangle?

11. What is the area of the isosceles
(37, 62)   triangle?

12. Evaluate: $ab - (a - b)$
(52)   if $a = 0.6$ and $b = 0.4$

13. What number is 15% of 1200?
(60)

14. Complete this table.
(48)

Fraction	Decimal	Percent
$\frac{3}{8}$	**a.**	**b.**
c.	**d.**	14%

15. Use a unit multiplier to convert
(50)   9000 g to kg.

Solve 16–17.

16. $q + 26 = 42.6$
(Inv. 7)

17. $6n = 33$
(Inv. 7)

Simplify 18–20.

18. $4.6 \times 3\frac{1}{4}$ (decimal answer)
(35, 43)

19. $(-6) + (+3) - (-2) - (+5)$
(68)

20. $2\frac{2}{3} \div \left(3\frac{1}{3} \cdot 2\right)$
(26)

     Saxon Math Course 2

1. Write a proportion to solve this
(72) problem: If 12 math books weigh
40 pounds, how much would 21
math books weigh?

2. What is the average of the
(28, 34) 2 numbers marked by arrows on
this number line?

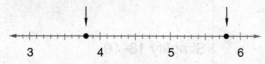

Refer to the trapezoid below for problems
3 and 4.

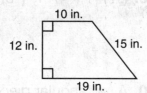

3. What is the perimeter of the
(19) trapezoid?

4. What is the area of the trapezoid?
(75)

5. Four squared is how much greater
(20) than the square root of 4?

6. Use a ratio box to solve this
(66) problem: Five hundred fifty
students attended the assembly.
If the ratio of boys to girls in the
assembly was 6 to 5, how many
girls attended the assembly?

7. Use a unit multiplier to
(50) convert 6.4 g to milligrams.
(1 g = 1000 mg)

8. Diagram this statement. Then
(71) answer the questions that follow.

*In the first fifth of the season the
Madrigals played 12 games.*

a. How many games did the
Madrigals play during the whole
season?

b. If the Madrigals won 60% of
their games during the whole
season, how many games did
they win?

Write and solve equations for problems
9 and 10.

9. Seventy-two is four fifths of what
(74) number?

10. One tenth of what number is 201?
(74)

15. Evaluate: $10m - (my - y^2)$
(52) if $m = 10$ and $y = 6$

11. Simplify:
(73)
  a. $-9(-2)$
  b. $-9(+6)$
  c. $\frac{-9}{-3}$
  d. $\frac{9}{-1}$

Solve 16–17.

16. $\frac{2}{3}m = 18$
(Inv. 7)

17. $n + 3.4 = 7$
(Inv. 7)

12. If each edge of a cube is 5 cm, what is the volume of the cube?
(70)

Simplify 18–19.

18. $3\frac{3}{4} \div \left(1\frac{2}{3} + 2\frac{1}{2}\right)$
(26, 30)

13. Find the circumference of each of these circles.
(65)

19. $(-7) - (-4) + (-3)$
(68)

 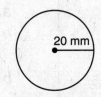

  a. Use $\frac{22}{7}$ for π.   **b.** Leave π as π.

20. A rectangular piece of metal swing
(67) around a rod. As it spins it sweeps
through a space the shape of a
  A. sphere
  B. cone
  C. cylinder
  D. pyramid

14. Complete this table.
(48)

Fraction	Decimal	Percent
$\frac{1}{6}$	**a.**	**b.**
c.	0.45	**d.**

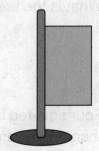

Saxon Math Course 2

Name _____

Score _____

1. Write a proportion to solve this
(72) problem: If 12 math books weigh
40 pounds, how much would 18
math books weigh?

2. What is the average of the
(28, 34) 2 numbers marked by arrows on
this number line?

Refer to the trapezoid below for problems
3 and 4.

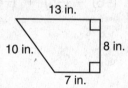

3. What is the perimeter of the
(19) trapezoid?

4. What is the area of the trapezoid?
(75)

5. Nine squared is how much greater
(20) than the square root of 9?

6. Use a ratio box to solve this
(66) problem: Five hundred fifty
students attended the assembly.
If the ratio of boys to girls in the
assembly was 7 to 4, how many
girls attended the assembly?

7. Use a unit multiplier to convert
(50) 4.6 g to milligrams.
(1 g = 1000 mg)

8. Diagram this statement. Then
(71) answer the questions that follow.

*In the first quarter of the season
the Matadors played 12 games.*

a. How many games did the
Matadors play during the whole
season?

b. If the Matadors won 75% of
their games during the whole
season, how many games did
they win?

Write and solve equations for problems
9 and 10.

9. Seventy-two is three fourths of
(74) what number?

10. One tenth of what number is 120?
(74)

11. Simplify:
(73)
   a. $-8(-3)$

   b. $-6(+3)$

   c. $\frac{-8}{-2}$

   d. $\frac{9}{-3}$

12. If each edge of a cube is 3 cm,
(70) what is the volume of the cube?

13. Find the circumference of each of
(65) these circles.

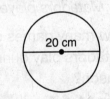

   a. Use 3.14 for π.   **b.** Leave π as π.

14. Complete this table.
(48)

Fraction	Decimal	Percent
$\frac{1}{12}$	**a.**	**b.**
c.	0.35	**d.**

15. Evaluate: $10m - (my - y^2)$
(52) if $m = 6$ and $y = 3$

Solve 16–17.

16. $\frac{3}{4}y = 12$
(Inv. 7)

17. $x + 2.6 = 5$
(Inv. 7)

Simplify 18–19.

18. $1\frac{7}{8} \div \left(4\frac{1}{6} - 2\frac{1}{2}\right)$
(26, 30)

19. $(-6) - (-5) + (-4)$
(68)

20. A triangular piece of metal swings
(67) around a rod. As it spins it sweeps
through a space the shape of a

   A. sphere

   B. cone

   C. cylinder

   D. pyramid

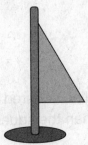

Name _____

Score _____

1. Tim mowed lawns for 2 hours and
(55) earned $7.50 per hour. Then he
washed windows for 4 hours and
earned $6.30 per hour. What were
Tim's average earnings per hour for
all 6 hours?

2. Evaluate: $x + (x^2 - xy) - y$
(52) if $x = 5$ and $y = 4$

3. Sketch an equilateral triangle.
(62)

Use ratio boxes to solve problems
4 and 5.

4. When Nasim cleaned his room
(65) he found that the ratio of clean
clothes to dirty clothes was 3 to 4.
If 35 articles of clothing were
discovered, how many were clean?

5. In 25 minutes, 400 customers
(72) entered the attraction. At this rate,
how many customers would enter
the attraction in 1 hour?

6. The diameter of a round skating
(65) rink is 15 m. Find the circumference
of the rink to the nearest meter.

7. The vertices of $\triangle ABC$ are A (1, 1),
(80) B (5, 1), and C (3, 3). Draw the
triangle and its image, $\triangle A'B'C'$,
translated 6 units to the left. What
are the coordinates of the vertices
of $\triangle A'B'C'$?

8. Graph $x > -5$ on a number line.
(78)

9. Natasha found that the 14 inches
(71) from her knee joint to her hip joint
was $\frac{1}{4}$ of her total height. What was
Natasha's total height in inches?

10. Simplify:
(73)

    A. $\frac{400}{-5}$

    B. $\frac{-7.2}{-6}$

    C. $15(-20)$

    D. $\left(\frac{1}{2}\right)\left(-\frac{1}{3}\right)$

11. Complete this table.
(48)

Fraction	Decimal	Percent
$\frac{5}{6}$	a.	b.
c.	0.6	d.

12. Find the area of this trapezoid.
(75) Dimensions are in meters.

Write and solve equations for problems 13 and 14.

13. Six hundred is $\frac{4}{9}$ of what number?
(74)

14. What percent of 40 is 30?
(77)

Solve 15–16.

15. $\frac{3}{5}m = 48$
(Inv. 7)

16. $1.5 = x - 0.08$
(Inv. 7)

Simplify 17–20.

17. $\frac{5\frac{1}{3}}{100}$
(76)

18. $\dfrac{3^3 + 2 \cdot 5 - 3 \cdot 2^2}{\sqrt{3^2 + 4^2}}$
(52)

19. $4\frac{2}{3} \div 1.4$ (fraction answer)
(26, 43)

20. $-2.6 - (-4.2) + (+3.5)$
(68)

Name _____

Score _____

1. Mai mowed lawns for 2 hours and
(55) earned $7.50 per hour. Then she
washed windows for 3 hours and
earned $6.25 per hour. What were
Mai's average earnings per hour for
all 5 hours?

2. Evaluate: $x + (x^2 - xy) - y$
(52) if $x = 5$ and $y = 3$

3. Sketch an isosceles triangle.
(62)

Use ratio boxes to solve problems
4 and 5.

4. When Meredith cleaned her room
(65) she found that the ratio of clean
clothes to dirty clothes was 2 to 5.
If 35 articles of clothing were
discovered, how many were clean?

5. In 25 minutes, 300 customers
(72) entered the attraction. At this rate,
how many customers would enter
the attraction in 1 hour?

6. The diameter of a round skating
(65) rink is 14 m. Find the circumference
of the rink to the nearest meter.

7. The vertices of $\triangle ABC$ are A (1, 1),
(80) B (5, 1), and C (3, 3). Draw the
triangle and its image, $\triangle A'B'C'$,
translated 5 units to the left. What
are the coordinates of the vertices
of $\triangle A'B'C'$?

8. Graph $x \geq -5$ on a number line.
(78)

9. Jason found that the 16 inches
(71) from his knee joint to his hip joint
was $\frac{1}{4}$ of his total height. What was
Jason's total height in inches?

10. Simplify:
(73)

   A. $\frac{300}{-5}$

   B. $\frac{-7.2}{6}$

   C. $15(-30)$

   D. $\left(-\frac{1}{2}\right)\left(-\frac{1}{3}\right)$

11. Complete this table.
(48)

Fraction	Decimal	Percent
$\frac{1}{9}$	a.	b.
c.	0.8	d.

12. Find the area of this trapezoid.
(75) Dimensions are in meters.

Write and solve equations for problems
13 and 14.

13. Six hundred is $\frac{5}{9}$ of what number?
(74)

14. What percent of 50 is 40?
(77)

Solve 15–16.

15. $\frac{3}{5}m = 45$
(Inv. 7)

16. $2.5 = x - 0.07$
(Inv. 7)

Simplify 17–20.

17. $\dfrac{6\frac{2}{3}}{100}$
(76)

18. $\dfrac{2^3 + 3 \cdot 5 - 2 \cdot 3^2}{\sqrt{3^2 + 4^2}}$
(52)

19. $1.4 \div 4\frac{2}{3}$ (fraction answer)
(26, 43)

20. $-2.3 - (-3.6) + (-1.5)$
(68)

Name _____

Score _____

1. The team's ratio of games won to
(53, 66) games played was 5 to 6. If the
team played 36 games, how many
games did the team fail to win?

6. Collect like terms:
(84) $3xy + xy - 4x + x$

Use ratio boxes to solve problems
7 and 8.

2. Find the **a.** mean, **b.** median,
(28, Inv. 4) **c.** mode, and **d.** range of the
following scores:

60, 70, 90, 70, 80, 65, 95, 80,
100, 60

7. If sound travels 2 miles in
(72) 10 seconds, how far does sound
travel in 2 minutes?

8. Before the clowns arrived, only
(81) 35% of the children had happy
faces. If 117 children did not have
happy faces, how many children
were there in all?

3. Elmo was chagrined to find that
(53, 66) the ratio of dandelions to peonies
in the garden was 11 to 4. If there
were 36 peonies in the garden, how
many dandelions were there?

9. Diagram this statement. Then
(71) answer the questions that follow.

*Forty-five thousand dollars was
raised in the charity drive. This
was nine tenths of the goal.*

a. The goal of the charity drive was
to raise how much money?

b. The drive fell short of the goal
by what percent?

4. Use a unit multiplier to convert
(50) 0.47 liter to milliliters.
(1 liter = 1000 milliliters)

5. Graph $x \leq -3$ on a number line.
(78)

 107

10. A certain rectangular prism is
(70) 4 inches long, 2 inches wide, and
3 inches high. Sketch the figure
and find its volume.

11. Find the area of this circle.
(82)

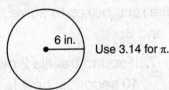

6 in.   Use 3.14 for π.

12. Complete this table.
(48)

Fraction	Decimal	Percent
$\frac{7}{20}$	a.	b.
c.	d.	6%

13. Multiply and write the
(83) product in scientific notation:
$(2.5 \times 10^6)(1.3 \times 10^9)$

Refer to the figure below for problems
14 and 15.

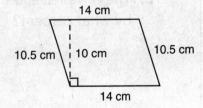

14 cm

10.5 cm   10 cm   10.5 cm

14 cm

14. Name this quadrilateral and find its
(19, perimeter.
Inv. 6)

15. Find the area of this quadrilateral.
(61)

Solve 16–17.

16. $15.4 = 1.4p$
(Inv. 7)

17. $z + \frac{4}{9} = 1\frac{1}{3}$
(Inv. 7)

Simplify 18–19.

18. $3\{25 - [7^2 - 4(11 - 4)]\}$
(63)

19. $(-3) + (-4) - (-7) + (-8)$
(64, 68)

20. Find the missing numbers in the
(56) table using the function rule. Then
graph the x, y pairs on a coordinat
plane and draw a line through the
points.

$$y = 2x + 1$$

x	y
0	☐
1	☐
2	☐

    Saxon Math Course 2

Name _____

Score _____

Cumulative Test 17B

Math Course 2
Also take **Power-Up Test 17**

1. The team's ratio of games won to
(53, 66) games played was 4 to 7. If the
team played 35 games, how many
games did the team fail to win?

2. Find the **a.** mean, **b.** median,
(28, Inv. 4) **c.** mode, and **d.** range of the
following scores:

50, 60, 80, 60, 70, 55, 85, 70,
90, 50

3. Milo was chagrined to find that the
(53, 66) ratio of dandelions to daisies in the
garden was 9 to 4. If there were
36 daisies in the garden, how many
dandelions were there?

4. Use a unit multiplier to convert
(50) 0.84 liter to milliliters.
(1 liter = 1000 milliliters)

5. Graph $x \geq -3$ on a number line.
(78)

6. Collect like terms:
(84) $4xy + xy - 3x + x$

Use ratio boxes to solve problems
7 and 8.

7. If sound travels 2 miles in
(72) 10 seconds, how far does sound
travel in 3 minutes?

8. Before the clowns arrived, only
(81) 45% of the children had happy
faces. If 110 children did not have
happy faces, how many children
were there in all?

9. Diagram this statement. Then
(71) answer the questions that follow.

*Forty-two thousand dollars was
raised in the charity drive. This
was seven tenths of the goal.*

a. The goal of the charity drive was
to raise how much money?

b. The drive fell short of the goal
by what percent?

Saxon Math Course 2   © Harcourt Achieve Inc. and Stephen Hake. All rights reserved.   **109**

10. A certain rectangular prism is
(70) 5 inches long, 2 inches wide, and
3 inches high. Sketch the figure
and find its volume.

11. Find the area of this circle.
(82)

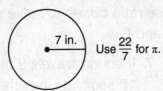

7 in.   Use $\frac{22}{7}$ for π.

12. Complete this table.
(48)

Fraction	Decimal	Percent
$\frac{3}{20}$	a.	b.
c.	d.	8%

13. Multiply and write the
(83) product in scientific notation:
$(2.4 \times 10^6)(1.5 \times 10^7)$

Refer to the figure below for problems
14 and 15.

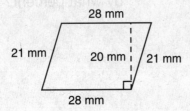

28 mm

21 mm   20 mm   21 mm

28 mm

14. Name this quadrilateral and find its
(19, Inv. 6) perimeter.

15. Find the area of this quadrilateral.
(61)

Solve 16–17.

16. $16.8 = 1.4p$
(Inv. 7)

17. $y + \frac{5}{6} = 1\frac{4}{5}$
(Inv. 7)

Simplify 18–19.

18. $2\{25 - [7^2 - 4(11 - 5)]\}$
(63)

19. $(-4) + (-5) - (-8) + (-7)$
(64, 68)

20. Find the missing numbers in the
(56) table using the function rule. Then
graph the x, y pairs on a coordinate
plane and draw a line through the
points.

$y = 2x - 1$

x	y
0	☐
1	☐
2	☐

Saxon Math Course

Name _____

Score _____

Math Course 2
Also take **Power-Up Test 18**

1. In the forest there were lions and
(54) tigers and bears. The ratio of lions
to tigers was 3 to 2. The ratio of
tigers to bears was 3 to 4. If there
were 9 lions, how many bears were
there? (*Hint:* First find how many
tigers there were.)

2. The shoe box was 25 cm long,
(70) 15 cm wide, and 8 cm high. What
was the volume of the shoe box?

3. If a coin is tossed and a number
(Inv. 8) cube is rolled, what is the
probability of getting heads and 6?

4. Use two unit multipliers to convert
(88) 81 square feet to square yards.

5. On a number line, graph the
(86) negative integers greater than −3.

6. How many degrees is $\frac{1}{6}$ of a full
(17) circle?

7. Diagram this statement. Then
(71) answer the questions that follow.

*Bill bought the shirt for $36. This
was $\frac{3}{4}$ of the regular price.*

a. What was the regular price of
the shirt?

b. Bill bought the shirt for what
percent of the regular price?

8. Use the information in the figure
(40) below to answer questions **a.** and **b.**

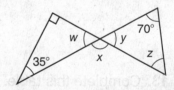

a. What is m∠w?

b. What is m∠z?

9. How many diagonals can be
(89) drawn from one vertex of a regular
hexagon? Illustrate your answer.

10. What is the circumference of this circle?
(65)

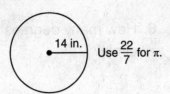

14 in.

Use $\frac{22}{7}$ for π.

11. Find the area of this trapezoid.
(75)

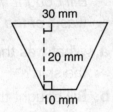

30 mm

20 mm

10 mm

12. Find the missing exponent.
(47)

$(10^3)(10^4) = 10^{\square}$

13. Complete this table.
(48)

Fraction	Decimal	Percent
a.	0.02	b.

14. What percent of 200 is 40?
(77)

15. Use a ratio box to solve this problem: Forty-five percent of the 5000 fast-food customers ordered a hamburger. How many of the customers did not order a hamburger?
(81)

16. Multiply and write the product in scientific notation:
(83)
$(1.25 \times 10^{-3})(8 \times 10^{-5})$

Solve 17–18.

17. $2\frac{1}{2}y = 75$
(Inv. 7)

18. $12.3 = 5.73 + f$
(Inv. 7)

Simplify 19–20.

19. $(-4x)(-2xy)$
(87)

20. $(-5) - (+6)(-2) - (-3)(-4)$
(85)

Saxon Math Course 2

Name _____

Score _____

1. In the forest there were lions and
(54) tigers and bears. The ratio of lions
to tigers was 2 to 3. The ratio of
tigers to bears was 4 to 3. If there
were 16 lions, how many bears
were there? (*Hint:* First find how
many tigers there were.)

2. The shoe box was 30 cm long,
(70) 15 cm wide, and 10 cm high. What
was the volume of the shoe box?

3. If a coin is tossed and a number
(Inv. 8) cube is rolled, what is the
probability of getting tails and 1?

4. Use two unit multipliers to convert
(88) 54 square feet to square yards.

5. On a number line, graph the
(86) negative integers greater than −4.

6. How many degrees is $\frac{1}{8}$ of a full
(17) circle?

7. Diagram this statement. Then
(71) answer the questions that follow.

*Jenny bought the shirt for $32.
This was $\frac{4}{5}$ of the regular price.*

a. What was the regular price of
the shirt?

b. Jenny bought the shirt for what
percent of the regular price?

8. Use the information in the figure
(40) below to answer questions **a.** and **b.**

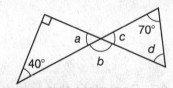

a. What is $m\angle a$?

b. What is $m\angle d$?

9. How many diagonals can be
(89) drawn from one vertex of a regular
pentagon? Illustrate your answer.

10. What is the circumference of this
⁽⁶⁵⁾ circle?

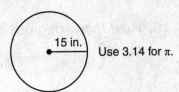

15 in.   Use 3.14 for π.

11. Find the area of this trapezoid.
⁽⁷⁵⁾

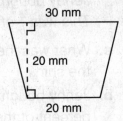

30 mm

20 mm

20 mm

12. Find the missing exponent.
⁽⁴⁷⁾
$(2^3)(2^4) = 2^\square$

13. Complete this table.
⁽⁴⁸⁾

Fraction	Decimal	Percent
a.	0.04	b.

14. What percent of 200 is 80?
⁽⁷⁷⁾

15. Use a ratio box to solve this
⁽⁸¹⁾ problem: Forty-five percent of
the 3000 fast-food customers
ordered a hamburger. How many
of the customers did not order a
hamburger?

16. Multiply and write the
⁽⁸³⁾ product in scientific notation:
$(2.5 \times 10^{-3})(4 \times 10^{-6})$

Solve 17–18.

17. $1\frac{2}{3}y = 75$
^(Inv. 7)

18. $12.5 = 1.25 + f$
^(Inv. 7)

Simplify 19–20.

19. $(2ab)(-3a^2b)$
⁽⁸⁷⁾

20. $(-3) - (+4)(-2) - (-2)(-6)$
⁽⁸⁵⁾

114

Saxon Math Course

1. After 3 tests Amanda's average score was 88. What score must she earn on her next test to have a 4-test average of 90?
(55)

2. Forty-five of the 80 students in the club were girls. What was the ratio of boys to girls in the club?
(36, 66)

3. Three dozen juice bars cost $4.80. At that rate what would be the cost of 60 juice bars?
(54)

4. There are 3 red marbles and 6 blue marbles in a bag. If Tad pulls out one marble and then another, what is the probability that both marbles in his hand will be red?
(94)

5. Because of the unexpected cold weather, the cost of tomatoes increased 50 percent in one month. If the cost after the increase was 60¢ per pound, what was the cost before the increase?
(92)

6. Write an equation to solve this problem: Sixty is what percent of 80?
(77)

7. Use two unit multipliers to convert 1000 cm² to mm².
(88)

8. If $x = -3$ and $y = 4x - 1$, then y equals what number?
(85, 91)

9. Find the volume of this prism. Dimensions are in centimeters.
(95)

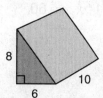

10. Complete this table.
(48)

Fraction	Decimal	Percent
$2\frac{1}{2}$	a.	b.
c.	d.	$2\frac{1}{2}$%

11. The price of the stereo was $96.00.
(46) The tax rate was 6%.

  a. What was the tax on the stereo?

  b. What was the total price of the stereo including tax?

12. Multiply and write the product
(83) in scientific notation:

$(7 \times 10^{-4})(4 \times 10^{8})$

13. Graph the whole numbers less
(86) than 3.

Solve 14–15.

14. $1\frac{2}{3}x = 60$
(90)

15. $3m - 45 = 54$
(93)

Simplify 16–20.

16. $(2 \cdot 5)^2 - 2(5)^2$
(63)

17. $(-3x)(2xy)(-xy^2)$
(87)

18. $4 - \left(2\frac{2}{3} - 1.5\right)$ (fraction answer)
(30, 43)

19. $3x + y - x + y$
(84)

20. $\dfrac{6 - 9 + 4 - 15 + 3(-4)}{2}$
(91)

Name _____

Score _____

1. After 4 tests Andrew's average
(55) score was 88. What score must
he earn on the next test to have a
5-test average of 90?

6. Write an equation to solve this
(77) problem: Sixty-four is what percent
of 80?

2. Fifty of the 80 students in the club
(36, 65) were girls. What was the ratio of
boys to girls in the club?

7. Use two unit multipliers to convert
(88) 10 cm² to mm².

3. Two dozen juice bars cost $4.80.
(54) At that rate what would be the cost
of 60 juice bars?

8. If $x = -4$ and $y = 2x - 1$, then
(85, 91) y equals what number?

9. Find the volume of this prism.
(95) Dimensions are in centimeters.

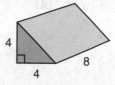

4. There are 4 red marbles and 6 blue
(94) marbles in a bag. If Sarah pulls out
one marble and then another, what
is the probability that both marbles
in her hand will be red?

10. Complete this table.
(48)

Fraction	Decimal	Percent
$1\frac{1}{2}$	a.	b.
c.	d.	$7\frac{1}{2}\%$

5. Because of the unexpected cold
(92) weather, the cost of tomatoes
increased 50 percent in one month.
If the cost after the increase was
90¢ per pound, what was the cost
before the increase?

11. The price of the stereo was
(46) $124.00. The tax rate was 6%.

   a. What was the tax on the stereo?

   b. What was the total price of the stereo including tax?

12. Multiply and write the product
(83) in scientific notation:

$$(8 \times 10^{-3})(2 \times 10^{10})$$

13. Graph the whole numbers less
(86) than 4.

Solve 14–15.

14. $3\frac{1}{3}x = 60$
(90)

15. $3w - 45 = 42$
(93)

Simplify 16–20.

16. $(2 \cdot 4)^2 - 3(4)^2$
(63)

17. $(-5xy)(x^2y)(3y)$
(87)

18. $6 - \left(2\frac{1}{3} - 1.5\right)$ (fraction answer)
(30, 43)

19. $3x - y - x - y$
(84)

20. $\dfrac{7 - 10 + 6 - 12 + 4(-3)}{3}$
(91)

Saxon Math Course 2

Name _____

Score _____

1. Jorge's average score on the first
(55) 3 tests was 88. His average score
on the next 5 tests was 84. What
was Jorge's average score on all
8 tests?

2. Use a ratio box to solve this
(92) problem: After working 6 months,
Gina received a raise of 25%. If
Gina's previous pay was $7.20 per
hour, what was her hourly pay after
the raise?

3. Write an equation to solve this
(77) problem: Seventy is what percent
of 50?

4. Use three unit multipliers to convert
(88) 2 m³ to cm³.

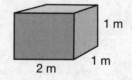

5. Diagram this statement. Then
(71) answer the questions that follow.

> *Five eggs were cracked. This
> was $\frac{1}{6}$ of the total number of eggs
> in the flat.*

a. How many eggs were in the
flat?

b. What percent of the eggs in the
flat were not cracked?

6. Evaluate: $\dfrac{a + b}{c}$
(91) if $a = -6$, $b = -4$, and $c = -2$

7. The perimeter of a certain square
(19, 20) is 12 inches. Find the area of the
square in square inches.

8. The face of this spinner is divided
(Inv. 8) into sixths. If the spinner is spun
twice, what is the probability that
the arrow will stop on a vowel both
times?

9. Find the volume of this triangular
(95) prism. Dimensions are in
centimeters.

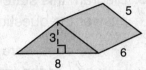

10. Find the area of this circle.
(82)

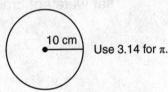

Use 3.14 for π.

11. Find the total cost, including 6%
(46) tax, of 20 square yards of carpeting
priced at $18.00 per square yard.

12. What is $33\frac{1}{3}$% of $42.00?
(60)

13. At 2:00 p.m. the hands of a clock
(7) form an angle that measures how
many degrees?

14. Multiply and write the product
(83) in scientific notation:
$(4 \times 10^3)(8 \times 10^{-8})$

Solve 15–16.

15. $0.6m + 1.5 = 4.8$
(93)

16. $\frac{2}{3}x - 6 = 18$
(93)

Simplify 17–20.

17. $3^3 - \sqrt{49} + 5 \cdot 2^4$
(52)

18. 3 yd 2 ft 9 in. + 8 in.
(49)

19. $2x + 3(x + 2)$
(96)

20. $\dfrac{-5(-4) - 3(-2)(-1)}{(-2)}$
(85)

Name _____

Score _____

1. Willis's average score on the first
(55) 3 tests was 84. His average score
on the next 5 tests was 88. What
was Willis's average score on all
8 tests?

2. Use a ratio box to solve this
(92) problem: After working 6 months,
Dana received a raise of 25%. If
Dana's previous pay was $6.40 per
hour, what was her hourly pay after
the raise?

3. Write an equation to solve this
(77) problem: Sixty-five is what percent
of 50?

4. Use three unit multipliers to convert
(88) 3 m³ to cm³.

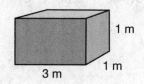

3 m   1 m   1 m

5. Diagram this statement. Then
(71) answer the questions that follow.

*Three eggs were cracked. This
was $\frac{1}{6}$ of the total number of eggs
in the carton.*

a. How many eggs were in the
carton?

b. What percent of the eggs in the
carton were not cracked?

6. Evaluate: $\dfrac{a + b}{c}$
(91) if $a = -8$, $b = -6$, and $c = -2$

7. The perimeter of a certain square
(19, 20) is 24 inches. Find the area of the
square in square inches.

8. The face of this spinner is divided
(Inv. 8) into sixths. If the spinner is spun
twice, what is the probability that
the arrow will stop on an odd
number both times?

© Harcourt Achieve Inc. and Stephen Hake. All rights reserved.

9. Find the volume of this triangular
(95) prism. Dimensions are in
centimeters.

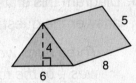

10. Find the area of this circle.
(82)

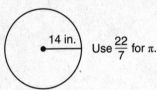

14 in. Use $\frac{22}{7}$ for π.

11. Find the total cost, including 7%
(46) tax, of 20 square yards of carpeting
priced at $16.00 per square yard.

12. What is $33\frac{1}{3}$% of $48.00?
(60)

13. What is the measure of the angle
(7) formed by the hands of a clock at
4:00 a.m.?

14. Multiply and write the product
(83) in scientific notation:
$(3 \times 10^4)(7 \times 10^{-9})$

Solve 15–16.

15. $0.6m - 1.5 = 4.8$
(93)

16. $\frac{2}{3}x + 6 = 18$
(93)

Simplify 17–20.

17. $3^3 - \sqrt{64} + 4 \cdot 2^4$
(52)

18. 2 yd 2 ft 7 in. + 8 in.
(49)

19. $4x + 2(x + 3)$
(96)

20. $\dfrac{-5(-4) + 3(-2)(-1)}{(-2)}$
(85)

122

1. The dinner bill totaled $24.00.
(46) Daniel left a 15% tip. How much
money did Daniel leave for a tip?

2. The 200-kilometer drive took
(46, 76) $2\frac{1}{2}$ hours. What was the average
speed of the drive in kilometers per
hour?

Use ratio boxes to solve problems 3–5.

3. The $\frac{1}{12}$-scale model of the rocket
(98) stood 48 inches high. What was the
height of the actual rocket?

4. Samantha saved $35 buying the
(92) suit at a 20%-off sale. What was
the regular price of the suit?

5. A merchant bought an item for
(92) $30.00 and sold it for 50% more.
For what price did the merchant
sell the item?

6. What is the sales tax on a $48.00
(60) purchase if the tax rate is 6.5%?

7. Find the perimeter of this figure.
(104) Use 3.14 for π. Dimensions are in
centimeters.

8. Use the Pythagorean Theorem to
(99) find *a*. Dimensions are in inches.

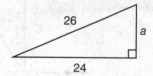

9. Find the surface area of this prism.
(105) Dimensions are in inches.

10. Find the volume of this cylinder.
(95) Use 3.14 for π. Dimensions are in centimeters.

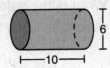

11. These two triangles are similar. Find x.
(97)

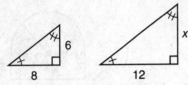

12. Find the measure of $\angle BOC$ in this
(101) figure.

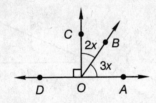

13. a. Arrange in order from least to
(100) greatest: 3, 3^2, $\sqrt{3}$, -3

b. Which of the numbers in part **a.** is irrational?

14. If John flips a fair coin twice, what
(Inv. 8) are the odds that the coin will land heads up twice?

15. Which of these numbers is betwee
(100) 7 and 9?

A. $\sqrt{8}$

B. $\sqrt{79}$

C. $\sqrt[3]{64}$

Solve 16–17.

16. $3x - 12 + x = 24$
(102)

17. $\dfrac{20}{w} = \dfrac{45}{3.6}$
(39)

Simplify 18–20.

18. $\dfrac{(2xy)(6x^2)}{3x^2y}$
(87, 103)

19. $3^2 + (-2)^3$
(20, 103)

20. $\dfrac{(-18) - (-2)(-3)}{(-2) + (-2) - (+4)}$
(85)

124

Saxon Math Course 2

Name _____

Score _____

1. The dinner bill totaled $18.00.
(46) Darryl left a 15% tip. How much
money did Darryl leave for a tip?

2. The 2100-mile flight took $3\frac{1}{2}$ hours.
(46, 76) What was the average speed of the
flight in miles per hour?

Use ratio boxes to solve problems 3–5.

3. The $\frac{1}{12}$-scale model rocket stood
(98) 30 inches high. What was the
height of the actual rocket?

4. Sarah saved $15 buying the dress
(92) at a 20%-off sale. What was the
regular price of the dress?

5. A merchant bought an item for
(92) $50.00 and sold it for 30% more.
For what price did the merchant
sell the item?

6. What is the sales tax on an $84.00
(60) purchase if the tax rate is 6.5%?

7. Find the perimeter of this figure.
(104) Use 3.14 for π. Dimensions are in
centimeters.

8. Use the Pythagorean Theorem to
(99) find *a*. Dimensions are in inches.

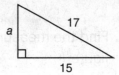

9. Find the surface area of this prism.
(105) Dimensions are in inches.

10. Find the volume of this cylinder.
(95) Use 3.14 for π. Dimensions are in centimeters.

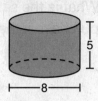

11. These two triangles are similar.
(97) Find x.

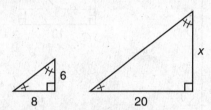

12. Find the measure of ∠BOC in this
(101) figure.

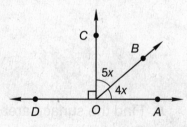

13. a. Arrange in order from least to
(100) greatest: 5, 5², √5, –5

b. Which of the numbers in part **a.**
is irrational?

14. If James flips a fair coin twice, wh
(Inv. 8) are the odds that the coin will lan
tails up twice?

15. Which of these numbers is betwe
(100) 5 and 7?

A. √6

B. √35

C. ∛27

Solve 16–17.

16. $2x - 12 + x = 24$
(102)

17. $\dfrac{30}{w} = \dfrac{45}{3.6}$
(39)

Simplify 18–20.

18. $\dfrac{(6x^2y)(4x^2)}{3xy}$
(87, 103)

19. $2^3 + (-2)^2$
(20, 103)

20. $\dfrac{(-16) + (-2)(-3)}{(-3) + (-2)}$
(85)

Saxon Math Course

1. Find the **a.** mean, **b.** median,
*(28.
Inv. 4)* **c.** mode, and **d.** range for the
following scores:

88, 92, 89, 95, 88, 90, 89, 88, 87, 84

2. If two cards are drawn from a
(94) normal deck of 52 cards, what is
the probability that both cards will
be hearts?

Use ratio boxes to solve problems 3–5.

3. Marla can exchange $200 for 300
(54) Swiss francs. At that rate, how
many dollars would a 210-franc
Swiss watch cost?

4. The bag was filled with red marbles
(66) and blue marbles in the ratio of
5 to 7. If there were 180 marbles in
the bag, how many were red?

5. During the off-season, the room
(92) rates at the resort were reduced
35%. If the usual rate was $120
per day, what was the off-season
rate?

6. Find the volume of this right
(95) circular cylinder. Use 3.14 for π.
Dimensions are in centimeters.

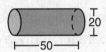

7. Use the formula $t = 1.06p$ to find
(108) t when p is 8.5.

8. Make a table that shows 3 pairs
*(Inv. 9,
107)* of numbers for the function
$y = 2x - 2$. Then graph these pairs
on a coordinate plane, and draw a
line through these points. What is
the slope of the graphed line?

9. What is the total price of an $80.00
(60) item plus 7.5% sales tax?

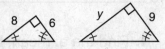

10. Ten percent of what number is 350?
(77)

11. Find the volume of this solid.
(105) Dimensions are in centimeters.

6 6 4 5

12. In this figure lines *l* and *m* are
(102) parallel. If m∠*a* is 105°, then what is
m∠*h*?

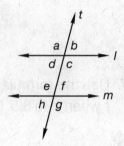

13. Solve the equation *d* = *rt* for *t*.
(106)

14. Find m∠*x* in this figure.
(40)

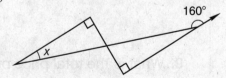

160°

x

15. The triangles are similar.
(97, 98)

8 6 *y* 9

a. Find *y*.

b. Find the scale factor from the smaller triangle to the larger triangle.

Solve 16–17.

16. $1\frac{2}{3}x - 15 = 45$
(93)

17. $3x - 12 = x + 24$
(102)

Simplify 18–20.

18. $\dfrac{(-6) - (7)(-4) - (-1)^2}{(-1) + (-2)}$
(85)

19. $100 - \{80 - 3[2 + 2(3^2)]\}$
(63)

20. $\dfrac{(-3ax)(4x^2)}{6ax^3}$
(87, 103)

 Saxon Math Course 2

1. Find the **a.** mean, **b.** median,
(28, Inv. 4) **c.** mode, and **d.** range for the
following scores:
93, 97, 93, 100, 94, 93, 92, 90

5. During the off-season, the room
(92) rates at the resort were reduced
35%. If the usual rate was $140 per
day, what was the off-season rate?

2. If two cards are drawn from a
(94) normal deck of 52 cards, what is
the probability that both will be
diamonds?

6. Find the volume of this right circular
(95) cylinder. Use 3.14 for π. Dimensions
are in centimeters.

Use ratio boxes to solve problems 3–5.

3. Hans can exchange $200 for 300
(54) Swiss francs. At that rate, how
many dollars would a 960-franc
clock cost?

7. Use the formula $c = 2.54n$ to find
(108) c when n is 4.

8. Make a table that shows 3 pairs
(Inv. 9, 107) of numbers for the function
$y = 2x + 2$. Then graph these pairs
on a coordinate plane, and draw a
line through these points. What is
the slope of the graphed line?

4. The jar was filled with peanuts and
(66) cashews in the ratio of 11 to 4. If
the total number of peanuts and
cashews in the jar was 630, how
many peanuts were there?

9. What is the total price of a $40.00
(60) item plus 7.5% sales tax?

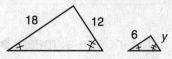

10. Ten percent of what number is 175?
(77)

11. Find the volume of this solid.
(105) Dimensions are in centimeters.

10 4
5
6

12. In this figure lines *l* and *m* are
(102) parallel. If m∠a is 115°, then what is
m∠f?

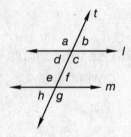

13. Solve the equation *d* = *rt* for *r*.
(106)

14. Find m∠x in this figure.
(40)

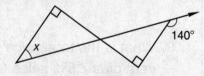

140°

x

15. The triangles are similar.
(97, 98)

18 12

6 y

a. Find *y*.

b. Find the scale factor from the
smaller triangle to the larger
triangle.

Solve 16–17.

16. $1\frac{2}{3}x + 15 = 45$
(93)

17. $3x - 24 = x + 12$
(102)

Simplify 18–20.

18. $\dfrac{(-6) + (7)(-4) - (-1)^2}{(-1) - (-2)}$
(85)

19. $100 - \{90 - 3[4 + 3(2^3)]\}$
(63)

20. $\dfrac{(-4xy)(6x)}{12x^2}$
(87, 103)

130

Saxon Math Course 2

Use ratio boxes to solve problems 1–3.

1. The regular price was $21.00, but
(92) the item was on sale for 30% off.
What was the sale price?

2. If 24 kilograms of seed cost $37,
(54) how much would 42 kilograms cost
at the same rate?

3. An item was on sale for 30% off the
(92) regular price. If the sale price was
$21.00, what was the regular price?

4. Divide 6 × 10⁶ by 3 × 10³ and
(111) write the quotient in scientific
notation.

5. The median of these numbers is
(28, how much less than the mean?
Inv. 4)
        1.5, 0.6, 0.7, 0.85, 5.3

6. Three cards labeled A, B, and C are
(94) placed face down on a table.

John picks one card and holds it,
and then picks a second card. Find
the probability that one of the cards
is an A.

7. Tim left $3000 in an account that
(110) paid 8% interest compounded
annually. How much interest did
Tim earn in 2 years?

8. What percent of $30 is $4.50?
(77)

9. An aquarium with the dimensions
(114) shown is filled with water.

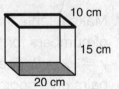

     10 cm
     15 cm
     20 cm

a. How many liters of water are in
the aquarium?

b. How many kilograms of water
are in the aquarium?

10. Use two unit multipliers to convert
(88)   4 ft² to square inches.

11. If Jan walks from point *A* to point
(112)   *B* to point *C*, she walks 140 yards.
How many yards would Jan save
by taking the shortcut from *A* to *C*?

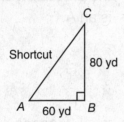

12. Find the volume of this pyramid.
(113)   The square base is 30 m by 30 m.
The height is 20 m.

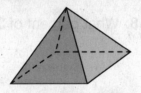

13. Make a table that shows 3 pairs
(Inv. 9, 107)   of numbers for the function
$y = -x + 2$. Then graph the number
pairs on a coordinate plane, and
draw a line through the points to
show other number pairs of the
function. What is the slope of the
graphed line?

14. Use the formula $A = \frac{1}{2}bh$ to find
(108)   *h* when $A = 20$ and $b = 10$.

15. Find m∠*x*.
(40)

16. Solve: $1\frac{3}{5}w - 17 = 23$
(90, 93)

17. Solve and graph on a number line
(93) $2x + 3 < 5$

Simplify 18–20.

18. $(-2)^2 \cdot 2^{-2}$
(52, 103)

19. $\dfrac{3x \cdot 3x}{3x + 3x}$
(87, 103)

20. $\dfrac{(-7) - (-3) + (2)(-3)}{(-3) - (2)}$
(85)

Name _____

Score _____

Use ratio boxes to solve problems 1–3.

1. The regular price was $21.00, but
(92) the item was on sale for 25% off.
     What was the sale price?

2. If 24 pounds of seed cost $41.00,
(54) how much would 42 pounds cost
     at the same rate?

3. An item was on sale for 25% off the
(92) regular price. If the sale price was
     $21.00, what was the regular price?

4. Divide 8×10^8 by 2×10^2 and
(111) write the quotient in scientific
     notation.

5. The median of these numbers is
(28, how much less than the mean?
Inv. 4)
     2.0, 0.6, 0.7, 0.85, 5.3

6. Three cards labeled A, B, and C are
(94) placed face down on a table.

Liz picks one card and holds it, and
then picks a second card. What is
the probability that one of the cards
will be a C?

7. Ming left $4000 in an account that
(110) paid 7% interest compounded
     annually. How much interest did
     she earn in 2 years?

8. What percent of $30 is $7.50?
(77)

9. An aquarium with the dimensions
(114) shown is filled with water.

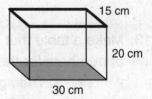

15 cm

20 cm

30 cm

a. How many liters of water are in
     the aquarium?

b. How many kilograms of water
     are in the aquarium?

10. Use two unit multipliers to convert
(88) 6 yd² to square feet.

14. Use the formula $A = \frac{1}{2}bh$ to find
(108) h when $A = 20$ and $b = 5$.

11. If Joan walks from point A to point
(112) B to point C, she walks 35 yards.
How many yards would Joan save
by taking the shortcut from A to C?

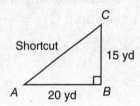

15. Find m∠x.
(40)

16. Solve: $2\frac{3}{5}y + 13 = 39$
(90, 93)

12. Find the volume of this cone. The
(113) diameter of the base is 20 in. Its
height is 15 in. Use 3.14 for π.

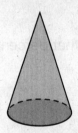

17. Solve and graph on a number line:
(93) $2x + 3 \geq 5$

Simplify 18–20.

18. $(-3)^2 \cdot 3^{-2}$
(52,
103)

19. $\dfrac{2x \cdot 2x}{2x + 2x}$
(87,
103)

13. Make a table that shows 3 pairs
(Inv. 9, of numbers for the function
107) $y = -x - 1$. Then graph the number
pairs on a coordinate plane, and
draw a line through the points to
show other number pairs of the
function. What is the slope of the
graphed line?

20. $\dfrac{(-7) + (-3) + (-2)(-3)}{(-3) - (-2)}$
(85)

134

Name _____

Test _____ Score _____

1.	2.
3.	4.
5.	6.
7.	8.
9.	10.

33333333333

33333333333

33333333333

11. **12.**

13. **14.**

15. **16.**

17. **18.**

19. **20.**

3

Saxon Math Course 2

Name _____

Test _____ Score _____

1.	**2.**
3.	**4.**
5.	**6.**
7.	**8.**
9.	**10.**

11.	12.
13.	14.
15.	16.
17.	18.
19.	20.

Saxon Math Course

Name _____

Test _____ Score _____

1.	2.	3.	4.	1.	
				2.	
				3.	
				4.	
5.	6.	7.	8.	5.	
				6.	
				7.	
				8.	
9.	10.	11.	12.	9.	
				10.	
				11.	
				12.	
13.	14.	15.	16.	13.	
				14.	
				15.	
				16.	
17.	18.	19.	20.	17.	
				18.	
				19.	
				20.	

Class _____

Class Test Analysis Form

Cumulative Tests

Student's Name	Cumulative Test			
	1	2	3	4
1.				
2.				
3.				
4.				
5.				
6.				
7.				
8.				
9.				
10.				
11.				
12.				
13.				
14.				
15.				
16.				
17.				
18.				
19.				
20.				
21.				
22.				
23.				
24.				
25.				
26.				
27.				
28.				
29.				
30.				

Saxon Math Course 2

Class _____

Cumulative Tests

Student's Name	Cumulative Test			
	5	6	7	8
1.				
2.				
3.				
4.				
5.				
6.				
7.				
8.				
9.				
10.				
11.				
12.				
13.				
14.				
15.				
16.				
17.				
18.				
19.				
20.				
21.				
22.				
23.				
24.				
25.				
26.				
27.				
28.				
29.				
30.				

Class Test Analysis Form A

Student's Name	Cumulative Test			
	9	10	11	12
1.				
2.				
3.				
4.				
5.				
6.				
7.				
8.				
9.				
10.				
11.				
12.				
13.				
14.				
15.				
16.				
17.				
18.				
19.				
20.				
21.				
22.				
23.				
24.				
25.				
26.				
27.				
28.				
29.				
30.				

Class Test Analysis Form A

Cumulative Tests

Student's Name	Cumulative Test			
	13	14	15	16
1.				
2.				
3.				
4.				
5.				
6.				
7.				
8.				
9.				
10.				
11.				
12.				
13.				
14.				
15.				
16.				
17.				
18.				
19.				
20.				
21.				
22.				
23.				
24.				
25.				
26.				
27.				
28.				
29.				
30.				

Class Test Analysis Form

Student's Name	Cumulative Test			
	17	**18**	**19**	**20**
1.				
2.				
3.				
4.				
5.				
6.				
7.				
8.				
9.				
10.				
11.				
12.				
13.				
14.				
15.				
16.				
17.				
18.				
19.				
20.				
21.				
22.				
23.				
24.				
25.				
26.				
27.				
28.				
29.				
30.				

Saxon Math Course

Class _____

Student's Name	Cumulative Test		
	21	22	23
1.			
2.			
3.			
4.			
5.			
6.			
7.			
8.			
9.			
10.			
11.			
12.			
13.			
14.			
15.			
16.			
17.			
18.			
19.			
20.			
21.			
22.			
23.			
24.			
25.			
26.			
27.			
28.			
29.			
30.			

Name _____

Individual Test Analysis Form

Cumulative Tests

Test Item No.	Cumulative Test Number											
	1	2	3	4	5	6	7	8	9	10	11	12
	Lesson Assessed											
1.	1	8	12	12	13	28	28	36	36	46	53	16
2.	2	7	13	13	12	28	12	28	28, Inv 4	28	55	53
3.	2	9	1, 12	8, 16	11	11	28	46	41	36	28	55
4.	5	10	11	14, 15	12	Inv 3	12, 35	22	38	28	8	41, 56
5.	4	4	12	5, 12	14, 22	22	19	35	Inv 3, 37	14, 43	22	60
6.	5	2	14	2, 9	Inv 2	19	22	35	22, 36	22	51	22, 36
7.	4	8	10	4	21	30	27	7	19	37	33, 35	57
8.	1	5	15	19, 20	15	16	33	32	40	43	50	Inv 6
9.	5	6	15	15	18	29	8	36	43	42	48	50
10.	3	9	6	9, 10	15	24	34	40	43	15	52	48
11.	3	3	7	15	3	30	Inv 3	34	42	19, 20	37	19
12.	3	3	8	20	3	27	34	31	42	39	19	37
13.	3	3	10	3	3	7, Inv 2	3	37	39	3, 35	3, 35	39
14.	3	9	15	3	23	21	31	35	3, 35	3, 35	39	3, 35
15.	3	9	1	15	10	3	35	35	3, 35	20	20	52
16.	1	9	1	9	23	3	35	23	30	49	52	20
17.	2	1	1	9	24	3	35	26	23	30	30	59
18.	1	1	2	9, 20	25	30	35	26	26	26	26	30
19.	1	9	3	20	20	30	9, 30	39	26	47	35	26
20.	1	7	3	2	7, 20	26	26, 30	3, 35	35	45	45	35

146

Saxon Math Course 2

Name _____

Individual Test Analysis Form B

Test Item No.	Cumulative Test Number										
	13	14	15	16	17	18	19	20	21	22	23
	Lesson Assessed										
1.	60	46	72	55	53, 66	54	55	55	46	28, Inv 4	92
2.	46	66	28, 34	52	28, Inv 4	70	36, 66	92	46, 76	94	54
3.	53, 66	65	19	62	53, 66	Inv 8	54	77	98	54	92
4.	28, 30	54	75	65	50	88	94	88	92	66	111
5.	60	35	20	72	78	86	92	71	92	92	28, Inv 4
6.	22, 48	22, 48	66	65	84	17	77	91	60	95	94
7.	57	67, 70	50	80	72	71	88	19, 20	104	108	110
8.	61	65	71	78	81	40	85, 91	Inv 8	99	Inv 9, 107	77
9.	32	69	74	71	71	89	95	95	105	60	114
10.	33, 45	37, 62	74	73	70	65	48	82	95	77	88
11.	64	37, 62	73	48	82	75	46	46	97	105	112
12.	48	52	70	75	48	47	83	60	101	102	113
13.	61	60	65	74	83	48	86	7	100	106	Inv 9, 107
14.	52	48	48	77	19, Inv 6	77	90	83	Inv 8	40	108
15.	39	50	52	Inv 7	61	81	93	93	100	97, 98	40
16.	3, 45	Inv 7	Inv 7	Inv 7	Inv 7	83	63	93	102	93	90, 93
17.	52, 63	Inv 7	Inv 7	76	Inv 7	Inv 7	87	52	39	102	93
18.	30	35, 43	26, 30	52	63	Inv 7	30, 43	49	87, 103	85	52, 103
19.	26	68	68	26, 43	64, 68	87	84	96	20, 103	63	87, 103
20.	35	26	67	68	56	85	91	85	85	87, 103	85

Saxon Math Course 2

Name _____

Score _____

Math Course 2
For use after Lesson 30

1. At Washington School there are 24 classrooms and an
(13) average of 25 students in each classroom. Which equation
shows how to find the total number of students (s) at
Washington School?

    A. $24 + 25 = s$ **B.** $24 \cdot 25 = s$ **C.** $24s = 25$ **D.** $25s = 24$

2. The Pilgrims founded Plymouth Colony in 1620. The American
(12) colonies declared independence in 1776. How many years
were there from the founding of Plymouth Colony to the
Declaration of Independence?

    A. 156   **B.** 256   **C.** 196   **D.** 154

3. Kwan went to the store with $20 and left the store with his
(11) purchases and $7.35. How much money did Kwan spend?

    A. $7.35   **B.** $7.15   **C.** $12.65   **D.** $27.35

4. Rolling a number cube once, what is the probability of rolling
(14) a number less than 4?

    A. $\frac{1}{2}$ **B.** $\frac{1}{3}$ **C.** $\frac{2}{3}$ **D.** $\frac{1}{6}$

5. Study this function table. What number is the output if the
(16) input is 2?

Input	Output
0	0
3	12
4	16
2	☐

    A. 4   **B.** 6   **C.** 8   **D.** 20

6. Three-fourths of the team's 28 points were scored in the first
(22)   half of the game. How many of the team's points were scored
in the first half of the game?

    A. 7   **B.** 14   **C.** 21   **D.** 28

7. Which of the following shows the prime factorization of 600?
(21)

    A. $2 \cdot 2 \cdot 3 \cdot 3 \cdot 5 \cdot 5$ **B.** $2 \cdot 2 \cdot 2 \cdot 2 \cdot 3 \cdot 5$

    C. $2 \cdot 2 \cdot 2 \cdot 3 \cdot 5 \cdot 5$ **D.** $2 \cdot 2 \cdot 3 \cdot 5 \cdot 5 \cdot 5$

8. The fraction $\frac{480}{600}$ reduces to
(15)

    A. $\frac{2}{3}$ **B.** $\frac{4}{5}$ **C.** $\frac{5}{8}$ **D.** $1\frac{1}{4}$

9. Which of these figures is a polygon?
(18)

    A.   **B.**   **C.**   **D.**

10. Which fraction below is equivalent to $\frac{7}{8}$?
(15)

    A. $\frac{15}{16}$ **B.** $\frac{50}{56}$ **C.** $\frac{63}{72}$ **D.** $\frac{49}{64}$

11. If $15x = 360$, then x equals
(3)

    A. $360 - 15$ **B.** $\frac{360}{15}$ **C.** $15 \cdot 360$ **D.** $360 + 15$

12. If $n - 36 = 24$, then n equals
(3)

    A. $24 + 36$ **B.** $36 - 24$ **C.** $24 - 36$ **D.** $24 \cdot 36$

13. Which set of fractions is arranged from least to greatest?
(8,
Inv. 1)

    A. $\frac{1}{2}, \frac{1}{4}, \frac{1}{8}, \frac{1}{16}$ **B.** $\frac{1}{2}, \frac{1}{16}, \frac{1}{8}, \frac{1}{4}$ **C.** $\frac{1}{16}, \frac{1}{8}, \frac{1}{2}, \frac{1}{4}$ **D.** $\frac{1}{16}, \frac{1}{8}, \frac{1}{4}, \frac{1}{2}$

Saxon Math Course

14. When new, Shayla's pencil was 7 inches long. Now her pencil
(23) is $5\frac{1}{4}$ inches long. How many inches of her pencil has Shayla
used?

A. $2\frac{1}{4}$ **B.** $1\frac{1}{4}$ **C.** $1\frac{3}{4}$ **D.** $2\frac{3}{4}$

15. Cheryl walked $1\frac{3}{10}$ miles to Maria's house. Then together they
(19) walked $1\frac{8}{10}$ miles to the park. How far did Cheryl walk to get
to the park?

A. $1\frac{5}{10}$ miles   **B.** $2\frac{1}{10}$ miles   **C.** $2\frac{5}{10}$ miles   **D.** $3\frac{1}{10}$ miles

16. There were $4\frac{1}{6}$ fruit pies in the restaurant desert case before
(23) dinner. After dinner there were $1\frac{5}{6}$ fruit pies in the case. How
many fruit pies were sold during dinner?

A. $3\frac{2}{3}$ **B.** $2\frac{2}{3}$ **C.** $2\frac{1}{3}$ **D.** $3\frac{1}{3}$

17. $\frac{4}{5} \cdot \frac{5}{6} \cdot \frac{3}{4}$ equals
(24)

A. 1   **B.** $\frac{1}{2}$ **C.** $\frac{1}{4}$ **D.** $\frac{1}{3}$

18. $\frac{2}{5} \div \frac{2}{3} =$
(25)

A. $\frac{4}{15}$ **B.** $1\frac{2}{3}$ **C.** $\frac{3}{5}$ **D.** $3\frac{3}{4}$

19. $10^2 - \sqrt{100} =$
(20)

A. 0   **B.** 10   **C.** 50   **D.** 90

20. Figure *ABCD* is a rectangle. Which segment is
(7) parallel to $\overline{AB}$?

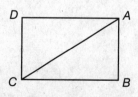

A. $\overline{BC}$ **B.** $\overline{DC}$ **C.** $\overline{DA}$ **D.** $\overline{CA}$

21. What is the area of this rectangle?
(20)

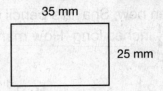

35 mm

25 mm

A. 60 mm   **B.** 120 mm   **C.** 245 mm²   **D.** 875 mm²

22. Andy rearranged and regrouped the factors in this expression.
(2)   What property of multiplication did Andy use to go from Line
1 to Line 2?

$$(1) \ 4 \cdot (7 \cdot 5)$$
$$(2) \ 4 \cdot (5 \cdot 7)$$
$$(3) \ (4 \cdot 5) \cdot 7$$

A. Commutative Property   **B.** Associative Property

C. Identity Property   **D.** Inverse Property

23. Which property of multiplication is illustrated by $\frac{3}{4} \cdot \frac{4}{3} = 1$?
(9)

A. Commutative Property   **B.** Associative Property

C. Identity Property   **D.** Inverse Property

24. What is the next number in this sequence?
(4)

$$1, 4, 9, 16, 25, \ldots$$

A. 30   **B.** 34   **C.** 36   **D.** 49

25. Which of the following is not illustrated by this 6 by 6 square?
(20)

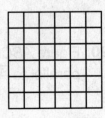

A. $6^2 = 36$ **B.** $\sqrt{36} = 6$ **C.** $36 \cdot 1 = 36$ **D.** $36 \cdot 2 = 72$

Saxon Math Course

1. The ratio of fiction to non-fiction books on the shelf was
(53) 2 to 3. If there were 60 non-fiction books on the shelf, how
many fiction books were there?

    A. 24   **B.** 36   **C.** 40   **D.** 80

2. The average age of three children in the Smith family is 11.
(55) If the first two children are 14 and 12, how old is the
youngest child?

    A. 10 years   **B.** 7 years   **C.** 5 years   **D.** 1 year

3. Amal traveled 78 miles by bus in 3 hours. What was the
(46) average speed of the bus in miles per hour?

    A. 75   **B.** 55   **C.** 62   **D.** 26

4. A coin is tossed and the spinner is spun. One possible
(36) outcome is heads and A (HA). Which choice below
shows the sample space for the experiment?

    A. {H, T, A, B, C}   **B.** {HA, HB, HC, TA, TB, TC}
    C. {HA, HB, TB, TC}   **D.** {HT, ABC}

5. Three fifths of the 60 vehicles were trucks. How many trucks
(22) were there?

    A. 12   **B.** 20   **C.** 35   **D.** 36

6. Ninety-three million in scientific notation is
(51)

    A. 93×10^7 **B.** 9.3×10^7 **C.** 90.3×10^6 **D.** 9.03×10^6

7. Which set of decimal numbers is arranged from least to
(33, 42) greatest?

    A. $0.6, 0.\overline{6}, 0.65$ **B.** $0.6, 0.65, 0.\overline{6}$ **C.** $0.\overline{6}, 0.65, 0.6$ **D.** $0.65, 0.6, 0.\overline{6}$

8. Which equation correctly shows how to convert 12 yards to
(50) feet using a unit multiplier?

    A. $12 \text{ yd} \times \frac{3 \text{ ft}}{1 \text{ yd}} = 36 \text{ ft}$ **B.** $12 \text{ yd} \times \frac{1 \text{ yd}}{3 \text{ ft}} = 4 \text{ ft}$

    C. $12 \text{ yd} \times \frac{1 \text{ yd}}{3 \text{ ft}} = 3 \text{ ft}$ **D.** $12 \text{ yd} \times \frac{3 \text{ ft}}{1 \text{ yd}} = 4 \text{ ft}$

9. Which choice below correctly shows both the decimal and
(48) percent equivalents for $\frac{3}{5}$?

    A. $0.25, 25\%$ **B.** $0.4, 4\%$ **C.** $0.4, 40\%$ **D.** $2.5, 250\%$

10. If a is 5, b is 4, and c is 3, then $ab - bc$ is
(52)

    A. 20   **B.** 12   **C.** 8   **D.** 2

11. What is the perimeter of this hexagon?
(19) (All angles are right angles.)

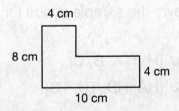

    A. 26 cm   **B.** 30 cm   **C.** 36 cm   **D.** 56 cm

12. Which equation best shows how to estimate
(29) the area of this rectangle?

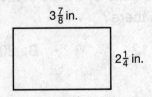

    A. $A \approx 4 \text{ in.} \times 2 \text{ in.}$ **B.** $A \approx 3 \text{ in.} \times 2 \text{ in.}$

    C. $A \approx 4 \text{ in.} \times 3 \text{ in.}$ **D.** $A \approx 4 \text{ in.} \times 4 \text{ in.}$

13. If $5.6 + w = 10$, then $w =$
(35)

    A. 5.4   **B.** 15.6   **C.** 4.6   **D.** 4.4

14. If $\frac{n}{6} = \frac{24}{18}$, then n equals
(39)

    A. 4.5   **B.** 8   **C.** 9   **D.** 144

15. $3^2 + 2^3 + \sqrt{36}$ equals
(20)

    A. 18   **B.** 21   **C.** 23   **D.** 35

16. $2 + 2 \times 2 - 2 \div 2$ equals
(52)

    A. 2   **B.** 3   **C.** 4   **D.** 5

17. $2\frac{1}{4} + 2\frac{5}{6}$ equals
(30)

    A. $4\frac{6}{10}$ **B.** $5\frac{1}{12}$ **C.** $4\frac{5}{24}$ **D.** $5\frac{1}{6}$

18. The shaded area of the grid illustrates that the
(26) product of $1\frac{1}{2}$ and $1\frac{1}{2}$ is

    A. 4   **B.** $2\frac{3}{4}$ **C.** $2\frac{1}{4}$ **D.** 3

19. What is the area of this rectangle?
(35)

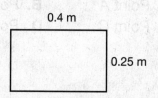

    A. 1 m²   **B.** 0.1 m²   **C.** 100 m²   **D.** 0.01 m²

20. 2.4 ÷ 0.08 equals
(45)

  A. 30   **B.** 3   **C.** 0.3   **D.** 0.03

21. There are 8 red marbles and 12 blue marbles in a bag. If one
(43) marble is drawn from the bag, the probability of drawing red is

  A. 0.8   **B.** 0.75   **C.** $0.\overline{6}$ **D.** 0.4

22. The missing exponent in $10^2 \cdot 10^4 = 10^\square$ is
(47)

  A. 2   **B.** 4   **C.** 6   **D.** 8

23. The area of this triangle is
(37)

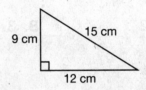

  A. 36 cm²   **B.** 90 cm²   **C.** 108 cm²   **D.** 54 cm²

24. If a truck driver can average 55 miles per hour, which equation
(54) shows how far the driver will travel in 4 hours?

  A. $d = 4 \text{ hr} \cdot 55 \text{ mi per hr}$ **B.** $d = \frac{55 \text{ mi}}{4 \text{ hr}}$

  C. $d = \frac{220 \text{ mi}}{4 \text{ hr}}$ **D.** $d = 55 \text{ mi per hr} + 4 \text{ hr}$

25. Which point has the coordinates (3, –2)?
(Inv. 3)

  A. Point *A*   **B.** Point *B*
  C. Point *C*   **D.** Point *D*

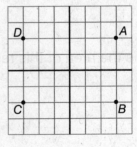

156

Name _____

Score _____

1. The ratio of rainy days to non-rainy days in April was 2 to 3.
(66) How many of the 30 days in April were rainy?

    A. 2 days   **B.** 20 days   **C.** 12 days   **D.** 18 days

2. This table shows the selling price of five real estate properties.
(28)

Selling Price

| $425,000 |
| $320,000 |
| $275,000 |
| $305,000 |
| $275,000 |

What was the median of these selling prices?

    A. $275,000   **B.** $305,000   **C.** $150,000   **D.** $317,000

3. In the first two hours of the trip Julissa drove 120 miles. In
(55) the next hour she traveled only 48 miles. What was Julissa's
average speed in miles per hour (mph) for the three-hour drive?

    A. 54 mph   **B.** 56 mph   **C.** 60 mph   **D.** 84 mph

4. A six-inch long pen is how many centimeters long?
(50) (1 in. = 2.54 cm)

    A. 8.54 cm   **B.** 10.16 cm   **C.** 12.7 cm   **D.** 15.24 cm

5. This graph illustrates the solution to
(78) which inequality?

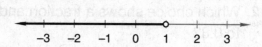

    A. $x > 1$ **B.** $x < 1$ **C.** $x \leq 1$ **D.** $x \geq 1$

6. $3xy + 2xy + 4x - x$ equals
(84)

    A. $5xy + 3x$ **B.** $5xy + 4$ **C.** $9x^2y$ **D.** $5x^2y^2 + 4$

7. If sound travels about 2 miles in 10 seconds, how far does
(72) sound travel in half of a minute?

    A. 30 miles   **B.** 15 miles   **C.** 10 miles   **D.** 6 miles

8. If 30% of John's photographs were perfect, but
(81) 210 photographs were not perfect, then how many
    photographs were there in all?

    A. 63   **B.** 300   **C.** 630   **D.** 700

9. When Julio finished reading page 180, he calculated that he
(71) was three-fourths of the way through his book. How many
    pages are in Julio's book?

    A. 240   **B.** 360   **C.** 135   **D.** 720

10. What is the volume of the shoe box?
(70)

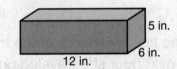

    A. 23 in.^{3} **B.** 180 in.^{3} **C.** 360 in.^{3} **D.** 720 in.^{3}

11. The area of this circle is
(82)

    A. 6π cm^2 **B.** 12π cm^2
    C. 36π cm^2 **D.** 9π cm^2

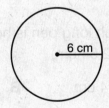

12. Which choice shows a fraction and a percent equivalent
(48) to 0.8?

    A. $\frac{1}{8}$, 8%   **B.** $\frac{8}{100}$, 8%   **C.** $\frac{4}{5}$, 80%   **D.** $\frac{1}{8}$, 80%

13. $(3.0 \times 10^6)(2.5 \times 10^5)$ equals
(83)

    A. 7.5×10^{30} **B.** 7.5×10^{11} **C.** 75×10^{11} **D.** 0.75×10^{11}

14. Which figure is not a parallelogram?
(Inv. 6)

A.    B.   C.   D.

15. What is the area of this quadrilateral?
(61)

A. 96 cm²   B. 108 cm²
C. 50 cm²   D. 42 cm²

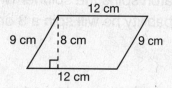

12 cm

9 cm   8 cm   9 cm

12 cm

16. If $1.2x = 14.4$, then x equals
(Inv. 7)

A. 1.2   B. 12   C. 17.28   D. 13.2

17. If $y + \frac{3}{5} = 1\frac{1}{10}$, then y equals
(Inv. 7)

A. $1\frac{7}{10}$ B. $\frac{3}{10}$ C. $\frac{1}{2}$ D. $\frac{4}{5}$

18. $2\{16 - [6^2 - 4(8 - 2)]\}$ equals
(63)

A. 32   B. 28   C. 8   D. 72

19. $(-2) + (-4) - (-6)$ equals
(64, 68)

A. 0   B. -6   C. -12   D. 4

20. The relationship between x and y shown in the table and
(56) graph is also shown by which equation?

x	y
-1	-2
0	0
1	2
2	4

A. $y = x - 2$ B. $y = 2x$ C. $y = 2x - 2$ D. $y = x + 2$

21. The diameter of Melia's bike tire is 24 inches. The
(65) circumference of the tire is about

    A. 50 inches   **B.** 75 inches   **C.** 100 inches   **D.** 450 inches

22. If Baron spins the spinner twice, what is the
(Inv. 8) probability he will spin a 3 on both spins?

    A. $\frac{1}{3}$ **B.** $\frac{1}{6}$ **C.** $\frac{1}{9}$ **D.** $\frac{2}{3}$

23. In triangle *ABC*, what is the measure of angle *A*?
(40)

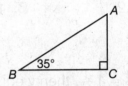

    A. 35°   **B.** 55°   **C.** 90°   **D.** 180°

24. If *x* equals 4 and *y* equals 3, then $xy - y^2$ equals
(52)

    A. 81   **B.** 12   **C.** 9   **D.** 3

25. One wall of an attic room is the shape of a trapezoid.
(75) The area of the wall is

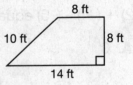

    A. 40 ft²   **B.** 56 ft²   **C.** 88 ft²   **D.** 112 ft²

Saxon Math Course 2

Name _____

1. 520 ÷ 25 equals
(1)

    A. 20.8   **B.** 28   **C.** 2.08   **D.** 2.8   **E.** None correct

2. 40.6 + 27.84 + 12 equals
(35)

    A. 32.02   **B.** 68.66   **C.** 80.44   **D.** 70.54   **E.** None correct

3. 3.8 − (2 − 0.18) equals
(35)

    A. 1.62   **B.** 1.98   **C.** 3.62   **D.** 3.48   **E.** None correct

4. 0.14 × 0.15 equals
(35)

    A. 0.21   **B.** 0.021   **C.** 0.0021   **D.** 2.1   **E.** None correct

5. 0.14 ÷ 70 equals
(35)

    A. 500   **B.** 0.02   **C.** 50   **D.** 0.002   **E.** None correct

6. $2\frac{1}{2} + 3\frac{1}{6} + 2\frac{1}{3}$ equals
(30)

    A. 8   **B.** $7\frac{3}{11}$ **C.** $7\frac{1}{2}$ **D.** $8\frac{1}{12}$ **E.** None correct

7. $5\frac{1}{6} - 3\frac{3}{4}$ equals
(23)

    A. $2\frac{5}{12}$ **B.** $1\frac{5}{12}$ **C.** $2\frac{7}{12}$ **D.** $8\frac{11}{12}$ **E.** None correct

8. $3\frac{3}{4} \cdot 3\frac{1}{3}$ equals
(26)

    A. $9\frac{1}{4}$ **B.** 15   **C.** $12\frac{1}{2}$ **D.** $1\frac{1}{8}$ **E.** None correct

9. $5\frac{5}{6} \div 2\frac{1}{2}$ equals
(26)

    A. $2\frac{1}{3}$ **B.** $2\frac{1}{2}$ **C.** $14\frac{7}{12}$ **D.** $\frac{3}{7}$ **E.** None correct

10. $\dfrac{24x^2y}{40xy^2}$ reduces to
(103)

    A. $\dfrac{3x}{8y}$ **B.** $\dfrac{3x^2}{5y^3}$ **C.** $\dfrac{3x}{5y}$ **D.** $\dfrac{4x}{10xy}$ **E.** None correct

11. Which digit in 50.143 has the same place value as the
(31) 7 in 6.8792?

    A. 5   **B.** 4   **C.** 1   **D.** 3   **E.** None correct

12. $(8 \times 10^3)(4 \times 10^4)$ equals
(83)

    A. 3.2×10^7 **B.** 3.2×10^{12}

    C. 3.2×10^5 **D.** 3.2×10^8

    E. None correct

13. One inch equals 2.54 centimeters. One foot equals how many
(88) centimeters?

    A. 30.48 cm   **B.** 25.4 cm   **C.** 21.8 cm   **D.** 12 cm   **E.** None correct

14. The formula $F = 1.8C + 32$ may be used to convert
(108) temperatures in °C (C) to °F (F). 30°C equals

    A. 54°F   **B.** 22°F   **C.** 86°F   **D.** −1°F   **E.** None correct

15. Which of these is NOT equivalent to 4%?
(48)

    A. 0.04   **B.** $\dfrac{4}{100}$ **C.** $\dfrac{1}{25}$ **D.** $\dfrac{2}{50}$ **E.** None correct

16. $\dfrac{2^4 \cdot 2^6}{2^2}$ equals
(20)

     A. 2^5 **B.** 2^8 **C.** 2^{12} **D.** 2^6 **E.** None correct

17. $\sqrt{5^2 - 3^2}$ equals
(52)

     A. 16   **B.** 8   **C.** 4   **D.** 2   **E.** None correct

18. Ten and two hundredths may be written as
(31)

     A. 210   **B.** 10.02   **C.** 0.102   **D.** 10.200   **E.** None correct

19. Estimate the product of $9\frac{5}{8}$ and $11\frac{2}{5}$ by first rounding each
(29) mixed number to the nearest whole number.

     A. 99   **B.** 108   **C.** 110   **D.** 120   **E.** None correct

20. Which set of numbers is arranged in order from least to
(33) greatest?

     A. −1, 0, 0.1, 1   **B.** −1, 0.1, 0, 1   **C.** 0.1, −1, 0, 1   **D.** −1, 0, 1, 0.1

21. What number solves this proportion? $\dfrac{2.4}{m} = \dfrac{3}{4.5}$
(39)

     A. 0.36   **B.** 3.6   **C.** 36   **D.** 360   **E.** None correct

22. The team's win-loss ratio was 5 to 3. If the team played
(66) 120 games without a tie, how many games did the team win?

     A. 75   **B.** 60   **C.** 45   **D.** 80   **E.** None correct

23. The average of Blanca's first three test scores was 90. The
(55) average of her next two test scores was 95. What was the
average of Blanca's first five test scores?

    A. 92　　　　**B.** 92.5　　　　**C.** 93　　　　**D.** 94　　　　**E.** None correct

24. Sam's first six scores were 90, 80, 90, 80, 80, and 100.
(Inv. 4) What is the median of these scores?

    A. 80　　　　**B.** 85　　　　**C.** 90　　　　**D.** 95　　　　**E.** None correct

25. One white marble, two blue marbles, and three red marbles
(94) were in a bag. One marble was drawn from the bag and
then put back. Then another marble was drawn. What is the
probability that a white marble was drawn both times?

    A. $\frac{1}{9}$　　　　**B.** $\frac{1}{12}$　　　　**C.** $\frac{1}{30}$　　　　**D.** $\frac{1}{36}$　　　　**E.** None correct

26. Dixon deposited $2000.00 in an account that paid 5% interest
(110) compounded annually. How much interest will the account
earn in two years?

    A. $105　　　　**B.** $200　　　　**C.** $205　　　　**D.** $210　　　　**E.** None correct

27. Greg drove 386 miles and used 20 gallons of gas. His car
(46) averaged how many miles per gallon?

    A. 19.6 mpg　**B.** 19.3 mpg　**C.** 193 mpg　**D.** 77 mpg　　**E.** None correct

28. At a 25%-off sale, a shirt cost $36.00. What was the regular
(92) price of the shirt?

    A. $45.00　　　**B.** $27.00　　　**C.** $48.00　　　**D.** $52.00　　　**E.** None correct

Saxon Math Course

29. Janice correctly answered 21 of the 24 questions. What
(81) percent of the questions did she answer correctly?

A. $87\frac{1}{2}$%   B. 84%   C. 90%   D. 78%   E. None correct

30. Jaime ran the first 2000 meters in 6 minutes. At that rate,
(54) how long would it take Jaime to run 5000 meters?

A. 9 min   B. 12 min   C. 15 min   D. 30 min   E. None correct

31. Which of these quadrilaterals appears to be a trapezoid?
(Inv. 6)

A.   B.   C.   D.   E. None correct

32. If $\angle x$ measures 140°, then what is the
(40) measure of $\angle y$?

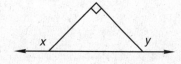

A. 140°   B. 40°   C. 50°   D. 130°   E. None correct

33. What is the perimeter of this figure?
(19) All angles are right angles.

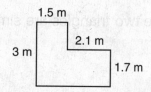

A. 13.2 m   B. 8.3 m   C. 11.9 m   D. 15 m   E. None correct

34. An arch in the form of a semicircle was
(104) over a 40-inch-wide doorway. Find the
length of the arch to the nearest inch.

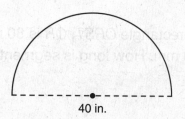

A. 120 in.   B. 100 in.   C. 63 in.   D. 48 in.   E. None correct

35. What is the total surface area of this cube?
(105)

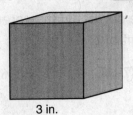

3 in.

A. 9 in.^{2} **B.** 27 in.^{2} **C.** 54 in.^{2} **D.** 81 in.^{2} **E.** None correct

36. The diameter of a circle is 12 in. What is
(104) the area of a 90° sector of the circle?
Use 3.14 for π.

A. 9.42 in.^{2} **B.** 28.26 in.^{2} **C.** 56.52 in.^{2} **D.** 113.04 in.^{2} **E.** None correct

37. What is the volume of this triangular prism?
(95)

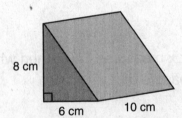

8 cm

6 cm   10 cm

A. 480 cm^3 **B.** 240 cm^3 **C.** 288 cm^3 **D.** 24 cm^3 **E.** None correct

38. These two triangles are similar. Find x.
(97)

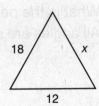

y   10   18   x

8   12

A. 15   **B.** 12   **C.** 9   **D.** 6   **E.** None correct

39. In rectangle *QRST*, *QR* is 30 mm and *RS* is
(112) 40 mm. How long is segment *QS*?

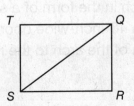

T   Q

S   R

A. 45 mm   **B.** 50 mm   **C.** 60 mm   **D.** 70 mm   **E.** None correct

40. In this figure, line *m* is parallel to line *n* and
(102) m∠a = 105°. What is the measure of ∠*g*?

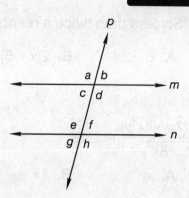

A. 105°   **B.** 85°   **C.** 75°   **D.** 120°   **E.** None correct

41. (−6) − (−7)(−4) equals
(85)

A. −52   **B.** −34   **C.** 34   **D.** −4   **E.** None correct

42. If $a = 3$, $b = 4$, and $c = -2$, then $b^2 - 4ac$ equals
(91)

A. 40   **B.** −8   **C.** 2   **D.** 8   **E.** None correct

43. $(-2)^3 - (-2)^2$ equals
(103)

A. −32   **B.** 4   **C.** −4   **D.** −12   **E.** None correct

44. Which choice shows the prime factorization of 500?
(21)

A. $5 \cdot 10^2$ **B.** $5^2 \cdot 2^3$ **C.** $2^2 \cdot 5^3$ **D.** $25 \cdot 20$ **E.** None correct

45. $3(x - 3)$ equals
(96)

A. $3x - 9$ **B.** $3x + 9$ **C.** $3x - 6$ **D.** $x - 9$ **E.** None correct

46. If $3.6n - 0.18 = 7.02$, then *n* equals
(102)

A. 0.2   **B.** 2   **C.** 1.9   **D.** 0.19   **E.** None correct

"Six less than twice a number" may be expressed as

A. $6 - 2x$ **B.** $2(x - 6)$ **C.** $2x - 6$ **D.** $x(2 - 6)$ **E.** None correct

48.
(103)
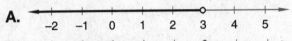
$\dfrac{(2xy)(4x^2y)}{8x^2y}$ equals

A. xy^2 **B.** $1x$ **C.** x^3 **D.** xy **E.** None correct

49. Which number line shows the solution of $2x - 1 < 5$?
(78)

A.
$$-2 \quad -1 \quad 0 \quad 1 \quad 2 \quad 3 \quad 4 \quad 5$$

B.
$$-2 \quad -1 \quad 0 \quad 1 \quad 2 \quad 3 \quad 4 \quad 5$$

C.
$$1 \quad 2 \quad 3 \quad 4 \quad 5 \quad 6 \quad 7 \quad 8$$

D.
$$1 \quad 2 \quad 3 \quad 4 \quad 5 \quad 6 \quad 7 \quad 8$$

50. This line represents what equation?
(107,
117)

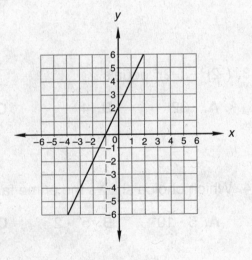

A. $y = x + 2$

B. $y = 2x - 1$

C. $y = 2x + 2$

D. $y = -2x + 2$

E. None correct

Saxon Math Course

Teacher's Notes

Teacher's Notes

Teacher's Notes

Teacher's Notes